The Spirit Of Polish History

Antoni ChoÅoniewski

THE SPIRIT
of
POLISH HISTORY

I.

ONE THOUSAND YEARS OF HISTORY

THE ANTIQUITY OF POLAND—TERRITORY—ROLE OF POLAND IN EUROPE—
INTELLECTUAL CULTURE—FALL OF THE STATE—LIFE OF THE COUNTRY
AFTER THE PARTITIONS

Poland, that today is being reborn to an independent life, is a country of ancient and noble traditions. Powerful and independent as early as the tenth century, Poland (at that time situated between the Vistula, the Oder and the Warthe Rivers) developed into a mighty State under the dynasty of the Jagellons, surpassing the other European states in area. From then on Poland extended from the Carpathian mountains to the Dwina River and from the Black sea to the Baltic. Under the successive reign of forty Kings, through the space of more than a thousand years, Poland developed her strength, placing it many times at the service of other countries and earning again and again titles of eternal glory.

Poland, situated on what was then the border of Eastern Europe—separating two different worlds—was the rampart that for hundreds of years safeguarded Europe and Christianity from the invasions of the Turks and the Mongols.

The long struggle against these barbarians, who menaced Europe, was begun in 1241 by King Henry the Pious at the battle of Lignica. Jan Sobieski, in 1683, struck the decisive blow to Turkish power under the walls of Vienna.

Europe could never have developed as it did, had not the barbarian invaders who had overrun Eastern Europe for five hundred years been checked by the victorious resistance of the Poles. In the middle ages the Lithuanians, the last pagan people of Europe, were converted to Christianity by the Poles who introduced the Bible and western civilization into their country.

The Polish people at that time had reached a high state of intellectual development.

In 1364, the first Polish University had already been founded at Cracow. It was the eminent forerunner of the Universities of Wilno, Warsaw, Lwow and Zamosc. The immortal Copernicus went forth from this ancient school. The XVI. century, that was the golden age of Polish culture, gave birth to illustrious poets, among whom Sarbiewski was crowned by the Pope, to eminent savants and to profound political writers. There was an efflorescence of great works brought forth from the new ideas of religious toleration, of the fraternity of peoples and respect for individual rights.

There was a new institution created at Warsaw, toward the middle of the eighteenth century, called the "Commission of Education." This was the *first* ministry of public education in Europe.

The reforms that this Commission introduced were based on principles far in advance of many of the ideas prevalent at that time.

A complicated political organization was created in Poland during that long period of progress. It was based upon lofty and daring historical conceptions and had peculiar characteristics. This organization more than all else has left a stamp of individuality on the past of Poland.

It is hardly a century since the Polish people, once so brilliant and powerful, were conquered in an unequal struggle.

Conquered yes, but *not* subdued.

Each generation in its turn, since the fall of the State, drawing the sword of its ancestors—the sword of the Kosciuszko's and the Poniatowski's—has striven to break the detested bonds.

In the life and death struggle for liberty, through these one hundred and twenty years, an uninterrupted series of revolutions have drenched Poland in blood. In its soul this people has always remained free, it has never accepted the outrages committed against it nor has it relinquished the rights that were torn from it.

Before the Chateau of Rapperswil, that shelters the Polish National Museum—the exiled Museum—there stands a memorial pillar, bearing the dates of each of the Polish insurrections, that proclaims to the world that the Polish soul can never be crushed and will protest forever agtinst this yoke.

Since the Confederation of Bar, since the first legions of Dombrowski mustered under the Eagles of Napoleon, this protest has been the watchword, the call transmitted from generation to generation up to the present day, when the world war has again brought forth the Legions of Poland.

Although deprived of independence for one hundred and twenty years Poland is still a homogenous people of twenty-five million souls, having a real historical individuality. This people that has withstood every misfortune, every defeat, is filled with a passionate desire to live. Notwithstanding the unthinkable oppression from which even the homes were not spared; notwithstanding the necessity of straining every force to protect the very foundations of existence; notwithstanding the terrible state of her bondage, Poland has given proofs of her capacity to develope, of her vital power in all domains of public life. She has competed with the world in her intellectual productivity; in the poetic inspiration of the genius of Mickiewicz; in the splendid prose of Sienkiewicz; in the magic of Chopin's work, that reveals the sorrow of this land; in the magnificence of the plastic art of Matejko and in the work of her savants who by their labors and by their researches have all contributed to lift the level of daily life.

A people having such a great and noble past, with such vital power, that has always collaborated in work for the good of civilization should be known to enlightened Europe, at least, well enough not to feel the need of an elementary course on this subject. However, this need is felt.

Poland, this living and real member of the European family that occupies, by the number of its population, the fifth place among the peoples of Europe, is only a very vague impression to the foreigner, with a value all but mystic. The reaction brought about by such a conception is sometimes a vague sentiment of sympathy (remnant of the time of the "heyday of peoples") but more often it is the reflection of prejudices, quite as vague, created by false ideas about Poland, ideas spread by those who have the historic tragedy of this country on their conscience.

It is from this more than suspicious source, that all along, such torrents of slander have flowed, tending to sully, in the eyes of the world, the noble and resplendent soul of the martyr—Poland.

The historians, especially the official Russian historians, who felt called upon to justify and sanction with servility the deeds that were done, heaped an avalanche of slander on the past of Poland, that little by little found its way through Europe and, because of the total ignorance of facts, the aim of this continual hawking of lies was finally accomplished. The historical truth of a series of common facts were completely distorted. It was thus that the belief in "Polish anarchy" was spread abroad, as well as that despicable story about different "oppressions" practiced in Poland.

What were the facts?

Let us leave aside the far off history of the middle ages and examine more closely the principal characteristics of the structure built up in modern times and that was called the "Polish Republic."

———o———

II.

THE CHARACTER OF SOCIAL LIFE IN POLAND

THE DEVELOPMENT OF ABSOLUTISM IN EUROPE AND THE EVOLUTION OF FREEDOM IN POLAND—SOCIAL AND POLITICAL LIBERTIES—THE PEOPLE AS A SOURCE OF POWER—THE ORGANIZATION OF THE STATE—THE PRINCIPLES—THE POLISH DIET AND ITS COMPETENCY—INTENSITY OF PUBLIC LIFE—THE REPUBLIC

At the close of the XVIth century Europe entered the period of modern absolutism. The idea of class autonomy, fruit of the preceding centuries, died out little by little, all over the continent.

The former State Diets, although their field of action had been greatly restricted, still represented the social element in power. Finally defeated after a long period of desperate struggle, they disappeared and made room for a new order of things. Those that remained here and there, simply as a matter of form, had no importance whatever. They passed away without having produced a higher form of organization.

Already in the XVIth century the Kings of France had been called "reges servorum," kings of serfs, instead of "reges francorum," and the political writers who sought for the difference between the "monarch" and the "tyrant" thought they had found it from the fact that the "tyrant shuns all contact with his subjects and fears the Diets (of whatever kind they may be) as a bat fears the light."

The new course of history tended more and more to group all the elements of government around the purple monarchy, so that in one hand, in the hand of the King-man, all the reins of power might be united, so that this man might be able to say, with pride: "l'Etat c'est moi!" In the XVIII. century, everywhere, with the exception of England and the republics of Holland and Venice, absolutism stretched out victoriously.

One will, having no responsibility, obeying no law, controlled peoples and States, as if they were private property. Before this blind force entire nations bowed down. Victorious autocracy reduced to nothing the part that the people had taken in public affairs and killed all interest in questions of public order.

In Poland things took an entirely different turn.

The organizations of Europe and of the Polish Republic evolved as differently as two streams running in opposite directions. There, around the throne, that mounted higher and higher, was formed the humble type of "narrow minded subject." Here, although the power passed more and more into the hands of the people, a type of free citizen was developed, who described his relations to the State by this proud maxim: "nil de nobis sine nobis."

From the XVth century the Poles developed their political and civic liberties with remarkable rapidity.

By the "Czerwinsk privilege" (1422) the nobility acquired the inviolability of property. From that time the King could not confiscate private property without legal proceedings.

In 1430 came the memorable law of the inviolability of the individual: "neminem captivabimus, nisi jure victum." This law guaranteed that no nobleman could be arrested without a legal warrant, except he be taken in the very act.

This Polish "habeas corpus act" preceded by several centuries the judicial conceptions of the European continent. This act, that was never violated, was later extended to the middle classes.

The "privilege of 1588" conferred the inviolability of the home. This act stipulated that a nobleman's house could not be subjected to a perquisition even though an outlaw were harbored in it.

Without special authorization a citizen of the Republic had the right to found societies and express his opinions either in words or writing. Under no circumstances could he be molested for having expressed an opinion on a political question.

The principles that are today called constitutional; inviolability of the individual, respect for private property and the home, liberty of association and religious toleration,—principles for which, in the XIX. century, such torrents of blood were shed in more than one country—were realized in Poland, in the XVth and XVIth centuries, and continued to be as long as the Republic existed, while in Europe injustice and iniquity ruled and the people were exposed to the despotic will of their masters.

Parallel with the individual rights, political rights developed. The starting point of the latter was the "Statute" of King Casimir Jagellon (statute of Nieszawa, 1454), according to which, the King agreed never to declare war, without the consent of the nobles united in provincial Diets (dietines). From that time on the nobles obtained access to legislative power. _The principle, that the people must be consulted on the obligations that they were expected to fulfill, grew more and more apparent, became the corner stone of the Polish state organization and the germ of the future parliamentary system.

Towards the end of the XVth century the periodic meetings of the nobles and Crown Counsellors were gradually transformed into "general Diets" that, henceforth, became an important and enduring factor in public life. The Diet was definitely organized in 1493.

In 1505 the Diet of Radom secured a legal basis for the organization and a new article was added to the fundamental statute: "nihil novi constitui debeat per nos, sine communi consensu conciliarorum et nuntiorum terrestium" (no decision shall be taken without the consent of the Council and the rural Deputies). This statute strengthened and developed the principle that all power must come from the people and that the people must obey the laws made by themselves through their representatives.

The general Diet constituted the legislative power of Poland and represented the entire nation. Like the English parliament it was composed of two chambers: the Senate and the Chamber of Deputies. The King was also a member, because of his legal status that conferred upon him the rank of "Estate".

Such a fusion of Royal power and national representation existed only in England, until recent times.

To enact a law the three factors or "executive Estates" (King, Senate and Nobility), were indispensable. Yet from the point of view of public law, neither the Senate nor the Chamber of Deputies alone, represented exclusively one of the estates because both churchmen and laymen sat in the Senate, while the Chamber of Deputies was made up (up to a certain time, at least) of members of the nobility and middle class.

The nobility was represented by deputies elected at electoral assemblies of "Dietines" while the urban deputies or "nonces" were elected by the middle classes.

The Diet decided upon the political life of the State: elaborated and proclaimed the laws and fixed the taxes, had jurisdiction, both penal and civil, over exceptionally important affairs, had control of the King and Government, had supervision of the administration and finances, had the direction of foreign policies, the right to make treaties and alliances and, it was the Diet that decided on peace and war. The Polish Kings could not declare war for personal or dynastic reasons. This supreme right belonged only to the people, and the people reserved the right to decide whether war or peace responded to their interests.

Few European parliaments have enjoyed such extraordinary privileges.

The meetings of the Dietes were always public. When the deliberations were finished the deputies were obliged to render accounts of the proceedings to their constituents, at special assemblies called "statement dietines."

Under such conditions political life developed with extraordinary intensity. The townspeople (middle class) however, soon left active politics using their franchise only to declare their nominal rights, while the landowners (nobility) took an ever increasing part in the political life of the country.

This political culture, that continued to develop without interruption for a considerable lapse of time, left its stamp on the Polish nobility. They were completely absorbed by the conduct of public affairs, that formed, as in the ancient Hellenic Republics, a favorite and honorable occupation and as in ancient Greece, had the power to impassion the minds of men. Everywhere, at the ordinary diets held every two years, at the special assemblies, at the innumerable provincial dietines, the elective tribunals, etc., etc., the nobles were occupied, either with local questions or affairs concerning the State.

This political development reached its maximum at the end of the XVIth century and remained as it was through the two following centuries, while almost the whole of continental Europe was under the yoke of despotism.

Since all of the nobility, composed of very numerous and very different elements, took part in the intensive political life, and since the throne had long ceased to be hereditary, Poland finally took on the characteristics of an aristocratic organization—aristocratic from the condition of her subjects actively interested in politics—but democratic and republican in practice.

———o———

III.

THE PEOPLE AND THE KING.

THE FREE ELECTION OF THE KING AND THE RIGHT OF ANY CITIZEN TO THE CROWN—RELATIONSHIP BETWEEN CITIZEN AND MONARCH—THE "ARTICLES OF HENRY OF VALOIS"—THE KING-PRESIDENT—RIGHT TO REFUSE OBEDIENCE—THE KING FOR THE PEOPLE AND NOT THE PEOPLE FOR THE KING

From the close of the middle ages, right up to the fall of the Republic, Poland recognized the principle that free men could not submit to authority that did not come from themselves. So, the King was not imposed on Poland by the blind chance of birth; he was freely chosen by an assembly in which every citizen, enjoying full right, could participate.

Besides the Senators and Deputies all the nobility of Poland, from the greatest magnate to the least important country squire, had the right to go to the "Diets of Convocation" and there, vote in person for the King. These elections were based on the principle of universal suffrage.

It is true that the nobility alone took part in the elections, but, being numerous, they really represented the will of the people.

The eligibility of the King, being the capital principle of Civic liberty, was watched over by this class with jealous care for centuries. But, threatened by the neighboring autocratic powers, the Poles were finally forced to adopt hereditary monarchy. And yet, of their own free will, the Polish people, during the long period of elective kings, chose seven successively from the Jagellon dynasty and later on three were chosen from the Wasa family and two from the Wettins. This fact simply proves that the people could and would conciliate their own political interests with those of the State.

The relationship existing between the people and their King showed clearly the character of the public institutions in Poland. The Polish gentleman justly appreciated the dignity of the King as a man and a citizen. "He *respected* the King," says the historian Kalinka, "as a moral authority, as a chief of the federation of nobles to which he himself belonged. But he had no fear of the King, for he never anticipated that his Sovereign would harm him in any way. It pleased him to be in the good graces of his King, but he could easily do without it, if necessary. What he was he did not owe to the King but to himself." In Poland there was not the shadow of

14

that byzantism and servility in intercourse with the monarch that characterized similar relations in Europe at the same time or even later.

The Pole was proud in the knowledge that he was not only an "elector" of Kings but that he had the right to the throne himself, and, in fact, the road to the throne was open to any member of the great community of nobles, if through his talents and merits he should be deemed worthy.

Four Kings were thus chosen in Poland and two of them, Sobieski and Leszczynski, are counted among her most excellent sovereigns.

Relationship with the King was in reality fixed by the constitution of the Republic. This constitution, to guard against the tyranny of one will, placed all power in the Diet and gave to each citizen the right to participate indirectly in the Government, and to the people, the responsibility of public affairs.

Royal power, as we have seen, was limited by the great authority of the Diet. From 1573 the Constitutional Statutes (called the "Articles of Henry") were presented to the King by the Elective Diet, upon his accession to the throne and also the "pacta conventa" that defined his royal power and drew the line so clearly between the rights of the King and those of the people. It was only after he had sworn allegiance to the Constitution, acknowledged the supreme power of the Diet and confirmed the national liberties that *the King* could take up his duties as first citizen of the State, a citizen who, notwithstanding the Royal title with which he was invested, was nothing more than the *President of the Republic.*

The manner in which the people guaranteed themselves against any autocratic attempt of the King was both simple and honorable. "If the King attacks the rights, the liberties, the articles and the pacts or if he does not hold to his engagements," stipulates the fundamental statute, "the citizens will be freed from their oaths of fidelity and obedience to the King."

This naturally, did not mean "errors due to human imperfections but to bad will and premeditated attacks against the liberty of the people" specified the Diet of 1576, "to the end that neither the King nor the citizens shall be in doubt on the will of the Republic." The law of 1609 "de non praestanda oboedientia" prescribed the exact preliminary procedure to be followed before being able to "definitely refuse obedience" to the King. For an act of such importance could not be carried out unadvisedly. If the King pub-

15

licly and in an undeniable manner attacked the laws to which he had sworn allegiance, he was to be given notice three different times by the Senate, then exhorted by the Archbishop. If he still persisted in his intent to harm the State, the Diet could use its right and annul the agreement. Thus, the loyalty of the people to their monarch was not unconditional. But as a remedy, to avoid abuse, the Polish law prescribed very severe punishments for anyone who created trouble under pretext that the King "premeditated the destruction of the Republic".

The article "de non præstanda obœdientia" shows to what an extent the law was venerated in Poland. It was set even above the King himself. It is to be remarked however, that these peculiar conditions did not hinder a King, with the strong moral cast of character of a Stephen Batory, to govern the people with an iron hand and inflict the death penalty on the most powerful magnates who were guilty of violating the law. The people seeing that he did not permit anyone to transgress the laws that he himself observed so scrupulously, upheld the King in such cases.

Such a bearing between King and citizens (not subjects) is hardly known in history. The Polish people settled their accounts with their King clearly and honestly, as free men. In all just demands the Government was answerable to the people and they, strong in this right, could call upon the Government to respect the law. The article "de non præstanda obœdientia" thus summed up the procedure for the annulment of the agreement between the King and the people.

"If thou wouldst grow old among us" declared the people to their sovereign, "respect our laws." Otherwise he would be obliged to return to his former condition but always surrounded by the respect due to his dignity and without drawing upon himself any kind of danger. The mask of the hired assassin never rose up before him in the dark shadow of night; poinard nor poison never threatened him. During the eight centuries of the existence of the Polish State, there was never a regicide. From the time of the very beginning of the power of the Diet, the nobles never ceased to oppose the introduction of the "dominum absolutum," that they saw spreading over Europe, and they always tried to prevent royalty from infringing upon their rights to the detriment of civic liberty. But never did the people drag one of their kings to the scaffold, nor never did one of their kings fall by the hand of an assassin. The Polish King never had to surround himself with guards but mixed fearlessly and freely with the people. Upon one occasion the heroic defender of Vienna, the popular Sobieski, did not hesitate to join in the wedding festivities of a humble blacksmith.

The sincere and knightly attitude that was characteristic of the Polish people in regard to their sovereigns grew out of the principle adopted in Poland, that "the King belonged to the people and not the people to the King". At this same epoch, the other peoples of Europe were becoming more and more subjected, more and more the property of their masters.

---o---

IV.

THE POLISH NOBILITY.

THE NUMBER—DIFFERENT RANKS: THE MAGNATES, THE "REDS," THE "MASS"—PECULIAR CHARACTERISTICS—EQUALITY OF THE NOBLES AMONG THEMSELVES—ENNOBLEMENT

To appreciate the historic past of Poland at its just value, one must remember that the nobility of this country was not formed of a very small proportion of the population as in other countries but, on the contrary, was made up of a very considerable part of it, more than in any other of the European countries. This high proportion of nobles was the specific characteristic of the organization of the Polish State.

While France, at the end of the eighteenth century, had only 140,000 nobles in a population of twenty million inhabitants (not even 1.5%), the Polish Republic at the same time could count one million (some historians say a million and a half) for every ten million inhabitants, that is to say 13% of the entire population. This high figure will not astonish us if we look for a moment at the structure of the Polish nobility.

Greatly differentiated, the categories of this nobility correspond, in a way, to a complete social organization. This "body", uniform in appearance, included three groups that were entirely different one from the other.

At the top were the great lordly families, the magnates, powerful proprietors, whose vast estates were larger than many of the small principalities of western Europe.

17

The rich landowners followed, a kind of English gentry, that was divided into two categories: one was composed of noblemen of old families called the "Crimsons" (Karmazyni) or "Purple Bearers", the other of families with smaller fortunes and of more recent nobility.

Toward the bottom of the ladder were the "small nobility", poor and very thickly settled, called "provincials" or "greys" (szaraczkowi). They owned, at most, a few acres of land and, not owning serfs, they were obliged to cultivate the land themselves. Economically these nobles differed little from the peasants and were even inferior to some of them—the peasants on the Royal domains, for example, who were not subject to forced labor.

At a still lower round of the ladder there were a multitude of gentlemen without any property whatever, who were simply called "Komornicy". These "Komornicy" worked in different capacities for the great landlords, attached themselves to the rich magnates or sometimes slipped into the cities, there to follow a trade or enter commerce.

The majority of the Polish nobility was made up of these working nobles, either with or without land. The creation of this nobility was due to different causes. Sometimes it happened that the entire dependent population of a village was ennobled, but more often they were the descendants of old and rich families who had become impoverished by the successive divisions of the land, through the right of descendants. There were also in this class, nobles who had been ruined by war or other calamities. As early as the XVI. century there were to be found in different parts of the Republic, in Masovia, in Lithuania, in Pomerania and in Podlasie, etc. etc., a numerous class officially called *nobiles pauperes,* the poor nobility, who little by little became assimilated with the peasants and who in the end, lost even their civil rights; villages and even entire districts were occupied by these *pauperes nobiles.* Even while tilling their bit of soil, these poor devils of noblemen, never left off the sword that was the sign of their high birth and proudly repeated to themselves the proverb, that so well characterized them: "with bare feet but with sword at side".

The fact that the Polish nobility was not a uniform class, but divided into many differnt groups, clearly differentiated it from western nobility. Also, the fact that this nobility formed such an immense part of the population was, as well, a phenomenon without analogy. So it was really not without some reasons, that the nobles, conscious of their privileged position and of their number, considered themselves not only a noble "class" but also a "people" of nobles.

All these different ranks of nobility—where the difference in fortune created such gulfs—were in reality equals. This "equality of all nobles" so proudly acknowledged, was one of the most remarkable traits of public life in Poland. From Radziwill, who could make Lithuania tremble,—down to the poorest wretch of the "grey nobility", all felt themselves to be equal, all being nobles. The most powerful Lord, who considered himself the equal of the King, would not think of addressing the most humble nobleman, without calling him "brother". The people have aptly expressed this in a favorite proverb, "the nobleman within his gates is the equal of the voivode".

In fact, before the law, save for a few insignificant exceptions, no difference existed between the several ranks of nobility. Their legal status toward the State was identical. The way into public affairs, honors and to the most exalted positions, not even excepting royalty, were open to every noble. The Poniatowski family is a striking example of this. The grandfather was a modest country squire; the son an eminent senator of the Republic; the grandson a King of Poland.

Any attempt to obtain titles of Baron, Count or Prince was absolutely prohibited by the nobility who thus safeguarded their equality. Each generation was reminded of this interdiction by many new laws and edicts enacted by the Diet that were inspired by the principle that there could be no greater honor than to be a citizen of the Republic.

The Polish King had no right to bestow titles on the nobility of the country but could only grant them to foreigners. The law of 1673 considered "defamed for life" any Pole who would accept a title from a foreign monarch and thus infringe the principle of equality.

The spirit of this "people of nobles" was republican and democratic in every sense of the word. Proud of their liberties that were not equaled on the continent, although sometimes allowing themselves to be carried away, this people was not exclusive and, except in the XVII. century when society became depraved by the Jesuits, they made no objections to the encroachments of new elements coming from other ranks of the population. It is a well known fact that whole villages were ennobled as the reward for military worth. Even the thirty thousand Tartars settled in Lithuania were given the liberties of nobility and admitted to military service while allowed to keep their Mohammedan religion.

After the victory of "Wielkie Luki" the Hetman Zamoyski bestowed his coat of arms upon the greater part of his soldiers. This example was followed by many other noblemen.

At the time of Sigismund 'August it was obligatory to ennoble a certain number of the middle class. The professors of the University of Cracow and the municipal officials of the principal cities, who were of plebeian origin, automatically obtained hereditary coats of arms. It was characteristic of the XVIII. century, that even the ennobling of Jews was allowed, baptized Frankists, an element that was scorned and despised at that time, to the greatest degree.

It has been clearly shown that public life was not carried on by a handful of despotic nobles, in possession of great liberties and exercising a decisive influence on the affairs of State, but by a great part of the people, a mass numbering millions. Two hundred thousand nobles presented themselves at the electorial urn. The significance of this figure is brought out by the fact that just before 1848 in post-revolutionary France, the rate of citizens who were authorized to elect their representatives was less than it had been three centuries before in Poand.

———o———

V.

THE UNIONS.

INTERNAL LIBERTIES, THE SOURCE OF THE POWER OF THE STATE—THE FORCE OF ATTRACTION—"THE FREE WITH THE FREE AND EQUALS WITH EQUALS"—THE UNIONS WITH PRUSSIA, LIVONIA AND LITHUANIA—THE FOUNDATIONS OF THE UNION WITH LITHUANIA—THE PRINCIPLE OF POLISH AUTONOMY—STATE PATRIOTISM—THE LASTING CHARACTER OF THE UNIONS

The internal organization, based on largely developed liberties, that so amply guaranteed the rights and the independence of her citizens, was bound to exert an influence on the surrounding peoples, and logically, bring about a greater development of the Polish State.

By following a course fundamentally Polish, not to be found elsewhere, by means of Unions with the neighboring States, Poland that was a comparatively small State at the time of the Piast kings, grew larger and larger. The neighboring peoples, subject to the severity of autocracy or arbitrary oligarchy, were attracted by the regime of right and liberty that the Polish people had instituted in their country, and manifested the desire to unite with Poland.

Through two centuries, from the beginning of the XV. to the end of the XVI. century, there was a long line of these unprecedented adhesions, until at last Poland became the largest State in Europe.

This is one of the most remarkable phenomena in history. It was not to brute force nor to the sword that Poland owed these glorious conquests. It was to her moral force and to the prestige of her laws. It was her liberties that drew to Poland these foreign territories and cemented these unions into an inseparable whole, that later gave proof of a cohesion rarely seen in the history of peoples. Poland in concluding the act of Union with Lithuania laid down the principle, immortal in its simplicity: "uniting the free with the free and equals with equals". The application of this principle brought about remarkable results. Kutrzeba, the Polish historian, points out with justice, that the Poland of the XVI. and XVII. centuries, running counter to the prevailing theories—according to which absolutism played the role of "cement" in State organizations—had been better able to unify the State, through the excessive development of democracy and its preponderance over royal power, than either Italy or Germany, for example, with their despotic governments.

In the XVIII. century Germany was composed of 250 small principalities. Territorially, Poland formed one uniform State. Brute force here had been replaced by a power far more effective: the power of love,—so literal was this that the first union with Lithuania was followed by at least a hundred marriages between the nobility of the two countries! A Union of love,—a kind of mystic marriage between two peoples—it was thus that they called the ultimate union between Poland and Lithuania. The act ratifying the union of Horodlo, 1413, began with this characteristic declaration:

"He shall receive no grace of salvation whom love does not sustain......It is love that creates laws, rules nations, builds cities and leads the republic to her best destinies, perfects all virtues of the virtuous......Therefore, we prelates, knights and nobility of the Polish crown by this document do unite our homes and future generations with the knighthood and nobility of Lithuania."

"It is a union without parallel," said Julian Klaczko, the illustrious Polish historian, "this union between two States so long hostile one to the other, and who, although different in race, in customs, in language and in religion, finally became united in the name of Christianity, of liberty, and of love that alone creates States". It is the first time in history that a great power was founded without the loss of a drop of blood.

"The Diet of Horodlo," declared the German historian Caro, "confirmed a union of peoples without precedent in the history of Europe."

In the annals of Poland there are many such achievements recorded. To all these peoples, to all these States, Poland left their oganizations, their language and their religion.

In 1454 the Prussian States,—where the cities were almost wholly German and the nobility was for the most part German or Germanized,—declared they would no more submit to the arbitrary government of the Teutonic Knights and demanded to be admitted into Poland. Twelve years later the union of Prussia with Poland took place. From 1466, Prussian Pomerania and the region of Danzig formed an integral part of the Republic but at the same time retained their own internal organizations.

The new province possessed its own jurisdiction called "Prussian corrections", also a Diet and treasury with a Prussian treasurer. Up to the very end of the Republic the Prussian deputies when affixing their signatures to the election decrees of the Kings never failed to add this clause: *"Salvis per omnia juribus terrarum Prussiæ"*. In Warmia, a district situated in Prussia where the Bishop was also Prince, there was still greater legal independence. On that annexed ground, German not only continued to be the official language of the municipalities but it was also used by the Royal Chancellor in his relations with the Prussian cities This rule was still observed two hundred years later by King Jan Sobieski who was, however, an ardent patriot.

In 1525, after the extinction of the Piast dynasty, the Duchy of Mazovia gave up its independence of it own free will and joined Poland. Here again the institutions and common law, known as the "Mazovian exceptions" were retained by the Mazovians for many years.

In 1560 Livonia sought to unite with Poland. Threatened by the growing power of Moscovy, Livonia that was governed by the "Knights of the Sword" could have had assistance from Sweden or Denmark, countries to which it was connected by race and religion. But this small, ecclesiastical State, although German and partly protestant, preferred to join Poland knowing full well that it was from there that the most complete autonomy would be obtained. And in fact, Livonia, incorporated into Poland, not only enjoyed full religious freedom but was also allowed to retain her own institutions and tribunals and, for a certain time, her Diet.

Gradually, without any pressure on the part of the Poles, a close union was formed with the Polish State and the German language that had been in use among the higher classes of Livonia was partly replaced by Polish.

In like manner to these three unions (Prussia, Mazovia and Livonia) the famous act of the Union of Lithuania and Poland was a work of the greatest importance not only because of the extent of the territory involved (Lithuania being almost as large as France), but also because of the historical value of such an act.

This work was accomplished by a series of conventions, extending over two centuries. Each of them drew the people closer and closer together. Thus this union was the result of a long evolution. There are three principal halting places that draw our attention in this long line of successive unions. The first of these occurred in 1386; it was a personal union through the accession of the Lithuanian Grand Duke Jagellon to the Polish throne and his marriage with the Polish Queen Jadwiga. In 1413 the union of Horodlo was concluded when the two peoples promised that the succession of the throne should always be settled by mutual accord. The nobility of the Grand Duchy of Lithuania then obtained liberties and political rights that had long been enjoyed by the Polish nobility.

After a lapse of 156 years (during that time the two peoples had the same dynasty) the third, last and real union was concluded at the Constituant Convention at Lublin, in 1569. The citizens of the two countries from that time on enjoyed equal rights and privileges. Lithuania was elevated to the same level as Poland and ruled by the same democratic principles.

The fundamental principle of the Federation, a common Parliament and King for the two countries, was definitely adopted. But each State retained its army, cabinet, treasury, local government, Civil and Criminal law.

Justice was rendered in the Lithuanian courts by a special code called the "Lithuanian Statute." It was stipulated in the act of the Lublin Federation that the native White Ruthenian should be the official language. How strictly and conscientiously the articles of Federation were observed is shown by the fact that the White Ruthenian language continued to be obligatory in official acts long after the nobility of the Grand Duchy of Lithuania, under the influence of Polish culture, had ceased to employ it. Thus the official life of the White Ruthenian language outlived its social life more than a century. From the time of the last union (1569) the rank of the two States was the same, but the bonds between them were so close that the inhabitants of the Grand Duchy of Lithuania as well as of Poland considered themselves above all citizens of the Republic.

The Federated Poland also gave autonomy to certain ethnographical groups not having a given territory. Thus, for example, the Armenians, who were scattered through the cities of southern Poland, had their own courts and laws, "the Armenian Statute." This statute, ratified by the Polish Parliament, settled all legal matters connected with the affairs of this commercial people.

For centuries the Jews had a perfectly independent social organization in Poland. The Jewish conventions met twice a year both in Lithuania and Poland. These conventions were composed of representatives of religious communities, and in their quality of "supreme court" decided different questions relative to Jewish autonomy. They were authorized to distribute the taxes, that the State levied in bloc, among the Jewish population. The Jews also had their own courts. A Jew would never accuse one of his co-religionists except before a court composed of Rabbies. It was only when a Jew accused a Christian or vice-versa that the affair was pleaded before the general court.

Thus, even the rights of those who lived here and there, scattered about in different cities and who did not own a foot of land were still recognized by the Republic.

One of the fundamental traits of the political regime of Poland was the spirit of toleration in the Constitution toward its many ethnical elements who differed in culture, language and race. Each well established ethnographical group enjoyed to the full the right to live and develop without hindrance.

On this ground, so favorable for liberalism, a kind of State patriotism developed in Poland, that was quite modern in type and in no way resembled the patriotism of other countries. The citizen was powerfully attached to the State by his political freedom and bound to appreciate this "serene Republic" that was his guarantee of freedom.

It was with truth indeed, that the eminent preacher of the XVII. century, Peter Skarga, could say: "Your country is not a step-mother to you, but a real mother; she folds you in her arms and allows no harm to come to you, while other States oppress and tyrannize their subjects."

The Polish nobleman, co-guardian of his country, proud of his freedom before the law, pitied his western neighbors, who scorned the peoples of the east, while they themselves were subject to autocratic governments. It was a consciousness of this remarkable situation, so different from that of the adjacent peoples that awakened in the hearts of all the population of this vast Republic a perception of their solidity and of their union, in spite of the differences in race, language or religion. From the Baltic to the Black Sea, in the midst of all these complicated ethnic elements, so heterogeneous (some elements approached Latin civilization and others Byzantine culture) one patriotic sentiment stood out clearly: love for the country belonging to them all; love for that country whose strength lay in the fact that the active political class, made up of all these heterogeneous elements, enjoyed entire civic freedom.

Through many successive generations history does not record any attempt to break up this splendid union of States and Peoples brought about by the genius of the Polish people.

The Federation of Poland and Lithuania, considering its political stability notwithstanding the diversity of its different elements, stands alone in the history of peoples. The union of Colmar (1397) —enacted between the Scandinavian States—lasted hardly a century. According to Dahlman, the Danish historian, the termination came because the union, based exclusively on principles of a material order, was the achievement of the sovereigns and not of the peoples. The Polish union has proved the imperishable nature of its deep foundation. How firmly Poland was able to unite the peoples she confederated and how permanent this union was is shown by the following fact: at the time when Poland officially ceased to exist the legal bonds that united her several peoples were broken, but they, nevertheless, continued to hold with her as before.

The Grand Duchy of Lithuania, the largest of these countries, has for more than one hundred and twenty years been a part of the Russian Empire, yet by the people who have played a political role, she considers herself joined to Poland. Every effort of Russia (she has not been sparing of them) to kill this sentiment has been fruitless. No pressure has been able to make the class that took part in the political life of Poland forget the past. For one hundred and twenty years Poland has been seconded by the Grand Duchy of Lithuania in her struggles for independence. At the time of the partitions and at the time of Kosciuszko's insurrection, Wilno took up arms. In 1831 blood flowed for the common cause in Lithuania as well as in Poland. In 1836 and in 1838 when Warsaw was benumbed into inaction by exhaustion, Lithuania arose again, and this time alone, against the detested Russian yoke. Thousands of Lithuanian revolutionists with their leaders, Konarski, Zawisza, Wollowicz, died martyrs for the restoration of the Republic.

A year before the insurrection of 1863 the two peoples met at Horodlo and in an immense procession, without parallel in the annals of nations, renewed in this memorable spot, the pledges of their eternal union. It is, indeed, impossible to separate all these elements that men or circumstances have long ago blended into an indivisible whole. It was Reytan, a son of Lithuania, who protested in the Parliament of Warsaw with such tragic despair against the partitions of Poland.

The man whose name has become the symbol of all Poland's highest aspirations, he who took the oath in the market place of Cracow to drive out the invaders, Thaddeus Kosciuszko, was a Lithuanian Pole. Adam Mickiewicz, the most forceful expression, the most eloquent exponent of the sorrows and desires of the Polish soul, poet of genius whose ashes repose in the Royal tomb on the Wawel, was also a Lithuanian Pole.

The descendants of those who in the long ago took the oath of allegiance to the one common Republic, the historic families of Radziwill, Sapieha, Czartoryski, and dozens, hundreds, thousands of other patriots are still faithful to the oath, conscious that they could never be other than one body and soul with Poland.

This is the most surprising phenomenon! The spiritual survival of a union, the Polish-Lithuanian, after the fall of the states that formed it. The spirit that prompted the acts of 1413 and 1569 lives on in the souls of the two peoples, although the acts are hidden away in some museum or library, although they are worthless and their executive power gone.

Such has been the resisting power of the judicious achievement of a Republic that united "the free with the free and equals with equals."

———o———

VI.

LIBERTIES AS A PREROGATIVE OF ONE LARGE CLASS OF PEOPLE.

A TRUE VALUATION OF THE LIBERTIES.—THE MIDDLE CLASS.—POLITICAL RIGHTS.—THE MUNICIPAL AUTONOMY IN POLAND.—THE SITUATION OF THE PEASANTS IN POLAND AND IN EUROPE, LEGAL AND DE FACTO.—REFORMS OF THE XVIII. CENTURY.—THE PSYCHOLOGY OF THE PEOPLE.—CONSTITUTION OF THE UNITED STATES AND SLAVERY.

The organization created by the Polish nobility was a model free State. But the official historians, contaminated by doctrinism, or even openly working for more or less suspicious interests, have affirmed over and over again that all this was of no value whatsoever, that Poland was a paradise for the governing class only, while the rest of the population lived under wretched conditions; that the peasants were oppressed and the middle class deprived of rights. To hear these crushing accusations denouncing this unequal division of rights, one might have thought that in Europe what were known as the lower classes, slept on beds of roses while in Poland they were oppressed by a regime of misery and servitude.

No! Every elementary book on history we take up will show that at that epoch the peasant was *everywhere oppressed;* that the middle classes were *everywhere deprived* of rights. During the last half of the XVI. century the agricultural population of Europe became more and more enslaved and the oppression grew to such an extent that the question was raised of which had the most enviable fate "the game that was carefully looked after and hunted but a short time or the subject who was never looked after and hunted all the time?"*

The middle class was also on the decline. They not only lost their civil rights but even the perquisites of their economic development. In the XVI. century, the nobleman in Germany—just as in Poland—in importing or exporting his agricultural products did not pay duty. The nobility, misusing this privilege, caused great harm to the industrial and commercial interests of the country by laying all the burden of the taxes on one class. Now, this phenomenon is generally admitted everywhere to have been an inevitable consequence of the conditions of historical development.

---

* Jansen, Geschichte des deutschen Volkes: "Was es besser habe. das lang gehegte und kurz gehetzte Wild, oder der stets gehetzte und nie gepflegte Unterthan."

No one would ever think of judging this phenomenon according to contemporary criterions. But for Poland there has been a singular exception made. The situation of the lower classes in the Poland of long ago is not judged by the ideas of that time but by the standards of the XIX. and XX. centuries. It then becomes very easy to anathematize the extraordinary exclusiveness of the nobility who so jealously safeguarded political rights from the other classes. With such sophistry we might be induced to regard Newton or Copernicus as dunces because they did not understand the phenomena that are evident to every school boy today.

Although the proper criterion of the political organization of Poland would be to compare it with thoughts and ideas prevalent at the time under consideration, still let us see if according to our present day notions the condition of the peasants, the middle classes and even the nobility in Poland was not better than in the neighboring States.

Although their social position had deteriorated, because of the privileges granted to the nobles and notwithstanding the fact that they had lost the greater part of the liberties acquired during the middle ages, still the middle class was not wholly deprived of rights, even political.

In the XVI. century the middle class of the Royal cities not only exercised judicial functions but had access to high dignities as well, and noblemen did not hesitate to call them "brothers".* We find in no place in the Polish Constitution a ruling that forbids the middle class from taking part in the Diet. In 1573 the "general Confederation" of Warsaw said: "We, the ecclesiastical and lay councillors of the Crown, all the nobility and other estates of the Republic one and indivisible".... The expression "other estates" has reference to the cities.

The principal cities, through their nonces, took part in all general assemblies or "Confederations", in all the Elective and Convocation Diets after 1573. Such cities as: Cracow, Vilna, Lemberg, Posen, Warsaw, Lublin, Kamieniec, Dantzig, Thoren and Elbing had the right to take an active part in the important act of electing the king: this right was exercised until the end. City representatives attended the Diet of 1668 to sign the abdication of John Casimir. In 1733 they ratified the "pacta conventa". These two acts took place during the time of the greatest development of absolutism among the

---

* Lozinski: "The patricians and the bourgeoisie of Lemberg in the XVI. and the XVII. centuries".

nobility and is a proof, as Grabiec, one of our historical writers, has observed, that it was above all, the indifference and inadaptability of the middle class that kept them from availing themselves of their civic rights.

Moreover, the spirit of caste that showed itself in the common law of Poland may be considered as a trait of degeneration.

During the XVII. and XVIII. centuries, that is at the period of the overlordship of the nobility, the number of cities doubled whose municipalities acquired the title of "nobiles" instead of the older "spectabiles et famati". The municipalities thus ennobled, on the ground of public organisms, became from that time on "legal persons" with rights equal to those of the nobility.

While in other countries the middle classes were unable to acquire land (until 1807 in Prussia), in Poland the inhabitants of all the large cities—Cracow, Lemberg, etc.,—had always enjoyed this right. As, on the other hand, it was comparatively easy to acquire the rights of townsmen, the right to own land had practically never been forbidden.

The difference that existed, is still more clearly shown in another field fully as important, that of city autonomy.

In the XVII. and XVIII. centuries the old city autonomies in many countries were either greatly limited or else rendered illusory as all the councillors and municipal employees were appointed by the monarch.

In Poland on the contrary, the municipal councillors were placed under the supervision of the royal "starosta" (Elder), but the internal organization of the councils was left intact. And, while elsewhere the legal and police service was more or less completely under royal control, these offices were always autonomous in Poland.

Finally, full autonomy, based on new principles was granted to the cities by the Constitution of May 3rd, 1791. It is thus that two totally different systems of government: that of centralization leveling in an autocratic sense almost the whole of Europe, and the Polish self government, so full of liberalism and exuberance, cast here their shadows and reflections.

Let us now examine the peasant class, the class that forms the greater part of the population.

At the time of the greatest extension of the political rights of the nobles, the Polish peasant—who during centuries had been free, subject only to the legal authority of the village mayor—fell into servitude under the patrimonial power of the overlord. A power that in time became unlimited.

Western Europe was on the same road and traveled so fast in that direction that she soon outstripped us. In Europe the sway of the nobility over the people began earlier than with us and the burden was far heavier because the oppression finally took on the nature of unbounded cruelty.

Notwithstanding the unhappy condition of the serfs, there however never were Princes in Poland who wore belts made of peasant skins; there never was known misery that caused the peasants to fly enmasse over the boundaries; the Polish Lord did not sell his people after the manner of the Lords of other countries—a thing that still happened in the XVIII. century in the middle of Europe; bloody revolts of the serfs, peasant wars followed by terrible suppressions, likewise the indescribable outbursts of despair among the rural class that fill the annals of Europe to overflowing,—all these were unknown in our country, on the contrary our annals expressly show that the peasants of all the neighboring countries, in order to make their lives easier, came and settled in Poland. At the time of the first partition of Poland, the Russians made mention of the so-called damage Poland had inflicted on her by giving refuge to 300,000 Russian peasants from the border districts.[1]

The peasants of Pomerania, Silesia and Moravia came in droves to Poland. In the XVIII. century when the *Austrian* government passed treaties for the *interchange of fugitives. Poland alone disclaimed the right of reciprocity, because her peasants never emigrated.*[2] During the time of the greatest subjection, the treatment received by the Polish peasants never reached the stage of cruelty, as it did in other countries. There is nothing to show that a Polish Lord, using his overlordship right, ever put his subjects to death. Moreover, serfdom did not last so long in Poland as it did in other countries of Europe; only during the XVII. and XVIII. centuries, for in the XVI. century the golden age of the peasants was still reflected from the two previous centuries. "The degree of subjection in Poland, and all its consequences, never reached the limits established here and there in Western Europe," said Oswald Balzer

---

[1] Thaddeus Lubomirski: The agricultural population of Poland.

[2] Grunberg: Die Bauerbefreiung in Boehmen. Maehren u. Schlesien. "Die Reciprocität scheint auch von diesen Ländern, mit Ausnahme Polens, gewährt worden zu sein, was sich leicht dadurch erklärt, dass wohl schlesische Unterthanen in grossen Massen nach Polen flüchteten, nicht aber umgekehrt".

who had a competent knowledge of the Polish organization. The peasant knew that, if on the one hand he had duties to perform, on the other he had rights; he knew he was under the protection of his overlord and that in case of misfortune (bad harvest, hail, etc.) he could count on a reduction in his rent, help through gifts of cattle, etc. Add to this, that the village institutions gave the peasant a certain degree of autonomy by allowing him to take part in the administration of current affairs. These decisions sometimes even acquired the force of a law.[1]

Neither must it be forgotten that a large part of the rural class, the peasants on the royal estates and in part those on the ecclesiastical domains, enjoyed certain civic rights and were under the protection of the State. Also there was a greater private initiative to improve the condition of the people in Poland than anywhere else. In this respect Poland had fine old traditions, for when the Republic was at the height of its development, in the *XVI. century*, the remarkable political writer, Andrew Frycz-Modrzewski, openly *called for the abolition of serfdom* and for *equal rights* for all classes.

At the beginning of the XVIII. century the King, Stanislas Leszczynski in his "Treatise on the Freedom of Speech" prepared the way for this idea of the necessity to emancipate the peasants from the legal, economic and cultural point of view. This *idea was taken up* by the whole of society, made rapid progress and gave remarkable results. Attempts to remodel the condition of peasant life on a modern basis were undertaken about 1740 on their great estates by many of the magnates: the Jablonowski, Brzoztowski, Zamoyski, Lubomirski, Potocki, Poniatowski, Czartoryski, Chreptowicz, etc. This movement became even more general in the latter part of that century. Serfdom was abolished; forced labor was replaced by tenure; the peasants were given personal liberties, autonomy, etc.

The result of these spontaneous reforms is to be seen in a tangible way from the fact that on the estate of Prince Stanislas Poniatowski alone, there were living some 400,000 peasants who were for the most part free and established as "landowners". "Without exaggeration," says A. Rembowski,[2] "one can affirm that in no other country of Europe was private initiative to renounce the rights of the privileged class carried so far as in Poland or so much good done for the peasants".

---

[1] Ulanowski: The jurisdiction of the Polish village during the XVI. and XVII. centuries.

[2] A. Rembowski: Comparison of State Constitutions.

)

The great reforms of May 3rd, 1791, improved the legal status of the peasants. Notwithstanding its imperfections it was so liberal in comparison with those which generally existed abroad, that the Russian Chancellor Bezborodko expressed fear that the "Polish epidemic" would spread and Leopold, Emperor of Austria, ordered the Governor of Galicia to work out a memorial on "what might be done for the peasants and middle classes after the reforms adopted in Poland".

Three years later, in 1794, the military leader Kosciuszko, in reality the popular dictator, made a great step in advance, when in his manifesto of Polaniec he proclaimed new decrees in favor of the peasants. This last political act of independent Poland, that regulated the status of the peasant class, gave them, among other things the protection of the government, the right of permanent abode, and other individual rights, victories that for that epoch were of great import.

Aside from these historical events the annals of Poland furnish us with psychological facts of equally great importance that characterize the relationship existing between the nobility and the people.

The old popular tradition attaches to the name of the last king of the Piast dynasty, the wise and good Casimir, the surname of "King of the Peasants", (a title accorded no other king in history) in memory of his solicitude in their behalf. This was the only King, among all the kings who through eight centuries occupied the throne of Poland, to whom the infallible instinct of the people attributed the title "Great"! In a country where the only "Great" king was at the same time the "King of the Peasants" the condition of the peasants must have been supportable even in the worst epochs.

A second psychological document still more profoundly expressive of the relationship existing between the nobility and the people was the devotion of the nobility to Kosciuszko. We have drawn attention to the fact that Kosciuszko inaugurated progressive reforms, that were, for the epoch, almost revolutionary. The leader of agonizing Poland in all his public efforts tried to give social justice to what is called the "lower classes". The companion in arms of Washington, after having taken part in the struggle for independence in America, after having been glorified by him as the "truest son of freedom", came back to Poland and took up arms against the invaders of the fatherland; he called the peasants to his standards; he continually manifested his democratic ideas and declared "that he was not fighting for the nobility alone but for the whole people". After the glorious battle of Raclawice, during which the peasants of Cracow, armed only with their scythes, took the Russian cannon by assault, Kosciuszko ostentatiously dressed himself in the "sukmana" * of the peasant, he the Dictator of the Republic where the nobles were masters. And, as all that did not dampen the enthusiasm of which Kosciuszko was the object, we may be sure that the gulf dug by history between the noblity and the people in Poland was not a very deep one.

Lastly, the innate gentleness of character that belongs to the Pole "dulcis sanquis polonarum", gentleness that had been remarked by foreigners in the XVI. century and because of which the Poles had always remained humane, even to their enemies, was the reason why there never was such oppression practised in Poland as by the nobility of other countries.

An example, the first one to mind; the supreme National Council that directed the last struggle against the invaders in 1794 declared to the people that "revenge on the enemy did not mean to direct their vengeance against a defenseless people, against prisoners, against any to whom they should guarantee security, but that vengeance worthy a Pole consisted solely in giving proof of courage".

In 1831, Warsaw, for the moment liberated, gave a striking example to humanity: the people gave relief to the prisoners of war, the wounded Poles gave up their places in the ambulances to wounded Russians and the National government supplied the necessary funds from the budget to provide a school for the Russian children remaining in Poland.

A nation that showed such humanity to an enemy could not have been cruel to their own people and so the hard laws that governed the life of the Polish peasants of long ago, were surely more tempered than exaggerated.

It is true that the freedom that was so greatly developed in Poland was restricted to the nobility alone. But still that fact cannot be used against the value of Polish freedom in general.

The fact of giving vast privileges to one class only of the population was a custom of the ancient Republics, that, even in our time, are everywhere considered as models of democracy and liberty. The same thing has happened in the United States of America, in quite recent times, where the Federal Constitution, one of the most liberal in the world, while conferring political rights on the white population did not abolish slavery among the negroes. "All men of color and

---

* A coat of homespun woolen cloth worn by the peasants.

their posterity, present and future, shall remain slaves forever and be subject to sale or gift equaling household goods and conforming to their nature," declares American law, the law of the country that had, however, already given birth to the immortal "Declarations of Jefferson. And these laws were not abolished until 1866 and only after terrible civil war. But no one because of this would be so absurd as to doubt the greatness of the political and social principles that proclaimed to the world the birth of free America, and that made it possible for America to outstrip the old Europe by nearly a century.

It is the same with Polish institutions. At the time when all classes in other countries were without political or civil rights while, on the contrary, at least one class in Poland, and that a very numerous class had rights; at the time when in all the countries of Western Europe the fate of the State depended on the will of one person, while in Poland a million inhabitants had the right to take part in the government, how illogical one must be and what ill-will one must show to deny without and against all evidence the high value of Polish liberties by alleging sophistically that these liberties were not enjoyed by the whole people.

VII

RELIGIOUS TOLERATION.

RELIGIOUS LIBERTY RESULTING FROM POLITICAL FREEDOM.—THE JEWS.—THE REFORMATION.—THE TOLERATION LAW (1573).—EQUAL RIGHTS GRANTED TO ALL RELIGIONS.—POLAND THE REFUGE OF THE PERSECUTED.—WHAT WAS THE ASPECT OF THE REACTION IN POLAND?—THE UNION OF BREST.

The cult of liberty—the source to which the Polish organization owed all its characteristic traits that favored the development of the different autonomies that were based either on historical or ethnical peculiarities—created religious toleration, carried it to a degree unknown in Europe and gave to it, at the time of it greatest vitality, a truly modern stamp.

We already know of the great freedom accorded to the Jews in Poland in the management of their private affairs. This same freedom was extended still farther into the more intimate domain of religious faith. In fact the Jewish religion always enjoyed the most complete liberty in Poland. Religious persecution, so ruthless elsewhere, was not known even by name in Poland, although through many distressing circumstances for the country the Jewish element, so different from the Armenian and Tartar element, gave evidence only of a very questionable loyalty to this most hospitable State.

Violence, of any nature whatsoever, was repugnant to the Polish character. Never were there "pogroms" in Poland. At the time of the most intense Catholic reaction the anti-jewish disturbances in Poland were but trifles compared with the frightful scenes of cruelty witnessed in Western Europe. Jewish blood was not shed in Poland. At no time were the Jews plundered and stripped of their property. Never were they driven out of the Polish cities. Even less were they obliged to submit to religious persecutions. The most flourishing centers of the Jewish cult were to be found in Poland.

"The Jews," states a Jewish paper* enjoyed a most magnanimous religious toleration and the greatest freedom during the entire existence of Independent Poland".

Thus religious fanaticism was ignored in Poland and every one was left free to worship God after his own fashion. These liberal ideas reached their height during the Reformation. The reform movement appeared very early in Poland and the Republic, attached by so many ties to the West and drawing so abundantly from the intellectual sources of Europe, made little opposition to the promulgation of new ideas.

Classic culture that was widely diffused among the upper classes had prepared the ground for religious reforms. A great many members of Poland's first families, the Radziwill, Leszcynski, Gorka, Olesnicki, Ostrorog, Firlej, Stadnicki, Zborowski, Laski, Tomicki and a great many others renounced Catholicism. The Archbishop Uchanski even had the design of founding a national church. Nicholas Rey, one of the great national writers, was drawn into this new current. Numberless non-conformist institutions: schools, printing houses, churches, etc., spread over the Republic; Calvinism and Lutheranism branched out more and more. Adepts of different sects and religions made their appearance in Poland; the "Bohemian Brothers", "Polish Arianism" and many others. Jan Laski, a Pole, undertook a proselyting journey and traveled as far as England, Friesland and Denmark.

---

* *Moriah*, December, 1916.

This great evolution of thought was accompanied by a spirit of toleration that not only existed nowhere else in Europe but that Europe many, times found difficult to understand. Western Europe burned "heretics" at the stake; blood flowed in streams "ad majorem Dei Gloriam"; thousands perished on the scaffold; others, hunted like wild beasts, fled from one country to another.

Poland knew little of the tortures of the inquisition. The Republic did no violence to the conscience nor did she stir up religious wars. The bloody persecutions of the dissenters was unknown in this Catholic country.

The people who created the creed of individual freedom in their political life could not be false to that principle in the spiritual domain of religion. Civic freedom, logically, gave birth to liberty of conscience and therefore to liberty of religion.

The Polish authorities immediately took a most liberal attitude toward the Reformation. In reality, religious freedom was established at the very beginning of the movement although it was not at first sanctioned by a constitutional clause.

During the XV. and XVI. centuries, although the Polish Kings, in their special decrees, always severely reproved the non-conformists for their "religious innovations", they left them in practice entirely free. We find Protestants among the highest dignitaries of the country. There were Protestants who presided over the Diet of the Republic. The fact of belonging to a religion other than Catholicism did not hinder in any way the fulfilment of public office. Moreover, even before the Reformation our attention is drawn to a significent fact: the wife of Alexander Jagello, Queen Helen, observed the Greek religion and had in the Chateau of Wilno her own private chapel.

At the time when different European Princes were steeped in the blood of their subjects who belonged to a different religion from their own; at the time when the principle "cuius regio, eius religio" put to shame this social condition, the great founder of the Union of Lublin, Sigismund August, the last of the Jagellon Kings, addressed to his people these memorable words: "I am not king of your consciences".

It was not long before the non-Conformists in Poland received a legal guarantee ensuring the free worship of their faith, and thus the liberty that they had already enjoyed was sanctioned. It was after this event that the Crown Chancellor, Jan Zamoyski, pronounced the words that show so well the state of mind of the

Polish people: "If it would lead you back to Catholicism I would gladly give up half of my life and with the other half I should live rejoicing in this union. But if anyone should try to compel you, then I would give up all my life, rather than be obliged to witness this compulsion".

The law relative to the liberty of conscience, decreed at the memorable Diet of Convocation in 1573, proves the large and generout spirit of the Republic and brilliantly shows the maturity and high development of the culture attained in Poland. At the time when fanaticism raged in the West, the Polish law "de pace inter dissidentes", enacted on January 28th, 1573, recognized the legal existence of all the professions of faith observed in the country and declared that none should be persecuted because of their religious convictions.

Thus, religious toleration was sanctioned by the constitution of the Republic and became one of the fundamental laws of the country. From then on every King upon his accession was obliged to swear allegiance to this new constitutional law, as well as to all the other laws that had been enacted before. This right was accorded to the peasants as well as to the nobility and middle classes. "That a peasant was forced to go to church or punished because he observed another religion that that of his overlord, that was never seen," declared a Polish writer of the XVII. century. *

Poland produced the effect of an absolute phenomenon at the time when the religious wars were drenching Europe with blood. The eyes of all those who suffered were turned to Poland, to the customs inspired by humane principles and the rights and liberties that this people enjoyed. Immediately after the Saint Bartholomew night the French Huguenots demanded of their King to "follow the example of Poland".

At the time of the great efflorescence of the Reformaton Poland became the asylum of the persecuted. Many foreign reformers: Ochino, Statorius, Stankar, Lismaninus, Socinius, Lelio and Faust driven from their own countries, came and continued their activity in Poland. Entire sects found protection and often new fields of endeavor. One part of the "Hussite" sect, the "Bohemian Brothers" driven from Bohemia in 1548, took refuge in great numbers in Poland. Again in the XVII. century, upon the decline of the spirit of toleration, great numbers of Germans, persecuted in their country,

---

* Rembowski: "The Confederation and the Revolt.

settled in the western part of the Republic along the Brandenburg and Silesian borders.

This state of things continued for two centuries. During the XVII. century, however, Catholicism gaining the upper hand, the liberties of the Protestants were restricted. But what was it in comparison with that which was happening in the rest of Europe? There were manifestations in certain cities, produced by strong religious tension, but without bloodshed.

These manifestations against which, moreover, special laws were enacted (Constitution on Troubles) never degenerated into civil war as in other countries.

That which is called the Catholic reaction in Poland was simply the return of many non-Conformists to the old faith. As for the fanaticism that was manifested during the last half of the XVII. and the first half of the XVIII. centuries, it consisted simply in the refusal to allow the building of new Protestant churches in the towns where the majority of the population was Catholic and restrictions of certain forms of the Protestant faith that were too demonstrative, and, lastly, the expulsion of the Arians, who were universally detested and suspected of carrying on traitorous relations with the enemy, that is with the Swedes. It is to be remarked, however, that the members of this abhorred sect were given two years in which to liquidate their private affairs.

The execution of the nobleman Lyszczynski, accused of atheism, religious murder ordered by the Diet of 1669, remained an isolated case. But, finally, the non-Conformists began to be eliminated from different offices and dignities, except in the cities, where up to the end they were still allowed to hold different positions.

But it is well to note the length of time it took for this reaction to develop; this slowness seems to prove without the shadow of doubt that it was not in harmony with the natural inclination of the nation.

During the whole of the XVII. century although the Catholic fanaticism made violent progress (because of the remarkable activity of the Jesuits) the political rights of the non-Conformists remained intact; until 1718 we see them as "nonces" in the Diet; until 1733 they sat on the bench as elective judges and filled other public positions.

Thus we see that the non-Conformists kept all their rights until the middle of the XVIII. century and hardly had they lost them (only for a very short space of time) when the new idealistic current made its way into Poland, the new "light" that brought in the reforms of the Great Diet (1788-1791).

The relatively short duration of the Catholic reaction in Poland and its slow advance is proof that the principle of religious toleration was profoundly inherent in the Polish character.

So it was in Poland, and only in Poland, that the difficult task of reconciling the two churches was brought to a happy conclusion: the Oriental and Roman Catholic churches. Work that was so often undertaken elsewhere without definite results.

Hardly thirty years after the union of Lithuania with Poland, in 1569, time of the beginning of the political unions, Poland succeeded also in bringing about the union of these two great factions of Christianity.

The union of the Greek and Roman churches was sealed at the Synod of Brest (Brzesc Litewski) in 1595. By this memorable act the Greek church while keeping its organization and peculiar rites, recognized the supremacy of the Pope. While the union of Florence (1439) had only an ephemeral existence and terminated in a new separation of the churches the union of Brest was so strong that when Russia tried to introduce the orthodox religion into the countries torn from Poland, when she tried to convert the "Uniates", she was obliged to have recourse to armed force (1874).

But still notwithstanding all the persecutions, these Uniates, of whom there are several million, continue to recognize the Pope as the head of their church.

———————o———————

VIII.

JURISDICTION.

THE DREAD OF COERCION.—THE MORAL TIES OF SOCIAL LIFE.—THE SENTI-
MENT OF RIGHT.—JURISDICTION.—PUBLICITY OF DEBATE AND DEFENSE.—
PROPERTY.—PUBLIC SECURITIES.—FOREIGN OPINIONS.

The evolution of the creative genius of political life in Poland, the organization of the country based on the principle: "No decision without our sanction", the freedom of elections, supported by the article concerning the refusal to obey the King, the unions, the autonomies founded on the principle of religious toleration,—all bring out the inherent characteristics of the Polish nature: the dread of coercion.

All of the great manifestations of the Polish people have been due to motives which were freely recognized and profoundly felt.

The bonds of the collective life to be conceded, had to have the moral sanction of all those belonging to the community. Valerian Kalinka, the great Polish historian, has thus characterized the Polish nobleman and his life: "Either as an official or officer he never considered himself an inferior but always as a voluntary fellow-worker; in private life as well, he was bound by tradition, faith, customs and hierarchy but as he recognized and admitted all these things of his own free will, he did not know or endure coercion".

Contrary to current theories according to which the State was looked upon as a compulsory organization, Poland was able to live through long centuries faithful to the ideas we have just stated.

In the XVI and XVII. centuries, Poland, "the powerful," also knew how to be aggressive: she entered Moscow two hundred years before Napoleon; she saved Christianity under the walls of Vienna and ended the power of the Turk. "And still," says Kalinka, "the whole organization of the Republic rested on the will of the citizen".

In reorganizing public administration, when the great reforms of May 3rd, 1791, were introduced, the Polish State created "civil and military commissions", that were the first manifestations of modern bureaucracy. But this bureaucracy had the same national characterictics that had dominated the previous epoch: every official considered it an honor to fulfill his civil duty as a citizen to the country and respect for the laws took the place of the discipline necessary in modern times.

This is what the distinguished historian, T. Korzon, says concerning this administration: "A study of registers, protocols and of divers dicisions, leads us to the conclusion that the working of the civil and military commission was entirely satisfactory to the authorities and population and that their decisions were accepted by all the community without compulsion.*

In the flourishing time of the Republic, during the XVI. and first half of the XVII. centuries, the mechanism of the Polish State moved smoothly notwithstanding the absence of all force. But during the following century the will of the citizen became insufficient to hold the State structure together under the same conditions.

This was the most unfortunate epoch for the Republic, the time of the Polish anarchy that was intentionally descried and blackened by the partisans of "salutary brute force".

---

* T. Korzon: History of Poland during the time of Stanislas August.

However, even in those trying times, that moral force, the sentiment of right, that had been manifested through the whole history of Poland, although enfeebled and sometimes degenerated, was still upheld by the people as a whole.

Moreover, this phenomenon is perfectly comprehensible. A people that had never had laws imposed by others, a people that had always been their own legislators, must, by the very nature of things, have succeeded in developing the sentiment of right to a higher degree than people whose every disposition to collaborate in the formation of the legal precepts, that govern social life, had been annihilated by the arbitrary will of the one to whom they were subjected.

One of the characteristic traits of Polish history is the complete absence of the period called "the law of might", the "Faustrecht" ("the mailed fist"). This "Faustrecht," the fruit of anarchy in the fullest sense of the word, that authorized everyone to resort to violence in any disagreement, was considered at certain times and places as the legal regime, there where tribunals and governments were unknown and the arbitrary exercise of justice was the privilege of all those who had at their command the supreme argument of force. Germany, notably, put the "Faustrecht", that had formerly served through several centuries, into force again during the thirty years' war.

Law was never so distorted in Poland. Anarchy was manifested in the Republic only by a few acts of violence organized by certain noblemen whose aims were to proceed with private executions of judgments rendered by the tribunals. On the other hand these "assaults" (Zajazd) that were very infrequent were always considered as "reprehensible violations of public law."

When anarchy was at its height, towards the middle of the XVIII. century, it was not rare to see the law severely applied: it was thus that the powerful Lithuanian magnate, Wollowicz, was condemned to death for his criminal adventures.

In all the judicial activity of Poland the pith and marrow of the two fundamental principles that served as a basis for the structure of the State, stand out: the cult of liberty and respect for the individual. This, more than all else, hastened the maturity of the political, legislative and judicial organization of Poland.

While in all European monarchies, except England, to make inquiry into a trial, they resorted to "inquisitorial proceedings, written and secret", to "confusing questions" and to torture, in Poland the procedure remained true to the principles of publicity and the spoken word for the debates of the accusation as well as for the defense. These principles were not introduced into Europe until the XIX. century under the influence of the great French Revolution, and before this revolution were applied only in England and in Poland. Favored by these principles the sentiment of right developed quite differently than with people subject to absolutism. It is sufficient to state one characteristic trait: the condemned man, of his own free will, went to prison to serve his sentence. In the case of his not giving himself up, he became an "exile" in the eyes of the world, a man outside of the law, who could be killed by any one with impunity.

How deeply the respect for the law was imbedded in the minds of the people may be seen from the fact that many times the Polish Courts of the XVIII. century, in handing down their decisions, even took their stand on clauses of the statute (Statute of Wislica) drawn in the XIV. century. The famous "mania for lawsuits" of the time of the decline, that was so fatal to the people, still shows, however, to what a degree the authority of the law was recognized. The *"law"* was always one of the favorite professions. It *was a national passion* like *agriculture* and the *army*. In fact, during the time of the great outbursts of passion, notwithstanding the mental abberations and regardless of the political troubles, the Poles perserved a profound cult for the idea of Law. "On this subject they are capable of becoming fanatics," remarked, in 1767, Repnine, the Russian ambassador who cordially hated the Poles. This respect for law was also manifested by the fact that the State Chancellor could refuse to affix the seal to an illegal or unconstitutional act, although ordered to do so by the King.

The respect for property was not only impressed on the minds of the nobility but on that of all the people. A popular saying alleged that it was "easier to lose one's life in Poland than his goods".

As to public safety, the touchstone of order in a political organization, we have the precious testimony of a foreign writer, Rulhiere,* who certifies that "Poland seems to be happy and quiet in the midst of the surrounding anarchy," that "safety prevails in the cities," that "travelers can go through the most lonesome forests or along the most frequented highways with all security," that "crimes are unheard of" and that "nothing can better confirm the theory of those philosophers who claim that man is by nature good".

---

* Rulhiere: History of Anarchy in Poland and the dismemberment of this Republic, (in French). Paris, 1807.

In 1779 a professor from Cambridge University, Cox, traveling with Lord Herbert, notes the fact that during all their journey through Poland nothing had been stolen from them, although their traveling carriage had alway been left in the street without a guard, while in Russia, never a night passed that something was not pilfered although a servant slept in the carriage.[1]

Another traveler, the German Biesler,[2] asserts that in Poland "One can move about with the greatest security even though having in one's possession thousands of ducats".

Schulz,[3] a Livonian, hostile to Poland, who lived in that country from 1788 to 1793, maintains that one must not believe what one hears about the insecurity of the highways in Poland. "I have crossed Poland three times; many of my friends have done likewise and never have we seen the least suspicious thing".

Add to these assertions the evidence of Thaddeus Korzon[4] who writes: "Each quarter, from the provinces of Posen, Cracow, Kamieniec, chests containing the fiscal circonscriptions amounting sometimes to a million florins were sent to Warsaw under the escort of one or perhaps two horsemen. That these treasure chests arrived so regularly at their destination is really a remarkable fact. After having examined all the acts concerning the activity of the Treasury Commission we are satisfied that during thirty years no transport was lost and that only once a chest was stolen by a band of Cossacks at Latyszow near the Turkish border".

"Since," remarks the same author judicially, "public safety is one of the aims of every penal system, and since this aim has always been attained in a manner worthy of admiration in Poland, it must be recognized that the Polish system had superior qualities before which many defects are obliterated."

———————o———————

---

[1] Cox: Travels into Poland. Russia and Denmark.
[2] Xavier Liske: Foreigners in Poland. 1791.
[3] Schulz: Reise eines Liefländers.
[4] Thaddeus Korzon: History of Poland during the reign of Stanislas August.

43

IX.

THE POLISH WARS.

AVERSION TO WARS OF CONQUEST.—THE KING PIAST'S SYMBOL.—THE LOVE
OF PEACE.—CUSTOMS.—MILITARY SERVICE, THE GENERAL LEVY.—THE PUR-
PORT OF THE POLISH WARS.—THE RAMPART OF EUROPE.—THE COMPETENCY
OF THE DIET ON WAR QUESTIONS.—THE EQUITABILITY OF WAR PROBLEMS.

Poland gave up the barbarous creed of war very early. As soon
as she passed out of the youthful period of her history she ceased the
pursuit of martial conquests. During the last five centuries of her
independent existence her growth was entirely due to her moral
force. The invasion of a foreign country, after the manner of
robbers, even under the cover of "State interests", was commonly
considered in Poland as cowardly. Arms were taken up only in
legitimate defense and this explains the characteristic name of
"necessity" ("potrzeba") that in olden times was given to war.

Stephen Buszczynski, speaking of the historical role of the
Polish people, dwells upon the fact that while other States almost
always owe their origin to the power of a conqueror or to the plun-
derings of a brigand chief, popular legend places near the cradle of
Poland a peasant king,—the legendary Piast,—symbol of labor, the
creator of peace. It is also to be noted that the title of "great" bestowed but once by the Polish people was not conferred upon one
of the many warrior kings, but upon a sovereign who made himself
memorable by his codification (the Statute of Wislica); who founded
the first university in Poland; who erected public monuments; who
built cities and who passed on to posterity with the praise of having
found "a wooden Poland and left one built of stone". It was this
architect-King, this King friend of labor and peace who alone received the title of "great": Piast and Casimir the Great, symbolized
all of Polish history.

The imperialistic desire to extend dominion "over all the earth",
that was the cause of such misery and so much bloodshed, was never
felt by the Polish people although this people was famous for its
legendary bravery. This tendency of domination was never mani-
fest in Poland not even when she was at the height of her power and
constituted one of the largest monarchies in Europe.

"In the midst of general robbery," says Julian Klaczko, "Poland
exempt from covetousness never monopolized the lands of others
even though she had every opportunity to 'rectify' boundaries or
undertake the role of providence."

44

The reply of the illustrious King, Sigismund "the Old", to those who offered him the crown of Hungary and Bohemia, "why wish to reign over several peoples when it is so difficult to contribute to the happiness of one", were memorable words that have many times proven true.

The Poles never sought to distinguish themselves in the warlike adventures that were of such common occurrence in the olden times. Choisnin, a delegate to Poland in 1573, wrote with the greatest admiration "this nation hates the spilling of blood except it be in open fight against declared enemies".

The Poles were aware of these peculiar traits of character and of the high moral level of their principles. It pleased them to cite the opinions that foreigners had of them: "dulcis est sanguis polonorum" and they added proudly: "abhorrent lectissimi et dulcissimi mores nostri abomni crudelitate, natura ipsa nostra ad omnem humanitatem facia, refugit ferocitatem".[1]

The army, from the remotest up to very recent times, was formed from a "general call to arms", the "pospolite ruszenie".

Defense was the only employment to which this army could be put and in consequence it could not be used outside national territory. Every citizen-noble was obliged to join this army and take part in the defensive wars, that alone were equitable in the eyes of the people. The middle classes were responsible for the defense of the cities.

A sharp lookout was kept on the accomplishment of this duty. In olden times the defaulters from military service were condemned to death and their property was confiscated, but the law of 1676 proscribed the latter punishment and in pursuance of this law the inheritance of all defaulters was added to the Treasury. It was only for very serious reasons that exemption from military service could be secured, and then only on the authorization of the Diet. The mercenaries, called "foreign troops", played a secondary role to the "general call to arms".

When, in the XVII. century, the whole of Europe was going through a military reorganization, forming large standing armies, excitedly reviving the art of strategy and of tactics and scientifically improving weapons the better to be able to destroy life, Poland did not allow herself to be drawn along in that current but contented herself with establishing the indispensable garrisons necessary to protect her frontiers and persisted in not maintaining a standing army in times of peace.

---

[1] Our cultivated and gentle manners loath cruelty, our very nature leans towards humanity, shrinks from ferocity. (Sobieski: "Les Huguenots").

The nobility fought with vehemence against the establishment of a standing army. They justly saw, that as they had not the spirit of martial conquest, such an army could only lead to a form of absolute power.

In 1788, however, because of the aggressive attitude of the neighboring powers, a decision was finally reached by the Diet, to raise and keep under arms a standing army of 100,000 men. Kosciuszko, the greatest strategist of contemporary Poland, in a memoire presented to the Diet, advised the organization of "militia", similar to the organization of the American militia, as it was in many ways similar to the Polish "general call to arms". He categorically opposed the formation of a standing army, saying that it would "put the citizens in irons".

Notwithstanding the aversion of the Poles to war and notwithstanding the imperfections and gaps in the system of the "general call", the history of the Polish army is full of glorious achievements. It was the Polish Knights who in the XV century, after a long series of terrible struggles, finally broke the greatest military power of contemporary Europe: the Teutonic Order, that under the sign of the Cross, gave themselves up to plunder and extortion. These Knights who had been called by Conrad, Prince of Mazovia, to convert the still pagan Prussians, established themselves on lands given them by this Prince, formed themselves little by little into a band of brigands and began a system of conquests even against their ancient benefactors, the Poles.

Hardly had the brilliant victory of Grunwald put an end to this pre-eminently defensive war against the Teutonic Order, when the Poles were obliged to turn to the East, where the Turks were menacing Europe.

Situated on the Eastern border of Europe, Poland, conscious of fulfilling her historic mission, threw herself into this new struggle, that was to continue for more than two centuries, for the defense of Christianity and Western civilization.

The young King Ladislas fell in the battle of Varna in 1444. From then on, especially after the fall of Hungary, the Polish Knights became imbued with the idea that they were really the living rampart chosen "to defend the Cross" against the "fanatical power of the Osmans". The task was brilliantly accomplished but only after the most terrible struggles. The exploits of the "winged Hussars", the flower of the Polish Army, were everywhere celebrated. From the steppes of Bessarabia and Hungary, even as far as the Balkans, the ground was covered with the graves of the Polish knights. For generations the greatest leaders of the Polish army began over and over again this traditional struggle and not only did they take part in the campaigns but they gave their lives as well on the battlefields. The great Hetman Stephen Zolkiewski, the "Knight without fear and without reproach", perished at Cecora in 1605. It was his great grandson, Jan Sobieski, who finally accomplished the destructon of the military power of the Turks.

So, even with their aversion to war and notwithstanding their "dulcis sanguis", the Poles were equal to the military problems of the day. Powerful and victorious, Poland used her strength to help her neighbors, not to overrun and pillage them.

She was, indeed, the rampart, the dike that protected Europe. The Poles always took up arms for ideals of which they were conscious and which they represented proudly.

Customs and ceremonies, both characteristic and beautiful, grew out of the high ideals the Poles had of the mission of their armies. He who sacrificed his blood and his life for his faith and his country was rewarded by a scarlet coffin. In the will made before his last expedition against the Turks, Hetman Zolkiewski charged: "If I fall on the field of honor cover not my coffin with black velvet, the sign of mournng, but cover it with red, the sign of joy".

In pursuance of an old Polish custom, during the reading of the Scriptures in church, every Knight, present, rose and drew his sword in sign that he stood ready to defend his faith whenever threatened. Faith was the Poles greatest boon at that time, and it was such lofty, spiritual motives alone that had power to arouse them to war.

Long ago in Poland, war depended on the will of the people, who expressed their judgment for or against it through their legally chosen representatives. The Diet alone could order a "general call to arms".

"The question so much discussed today," says Professor Stanislas Kutrzeba, "of whether the people as a whole (through their representatives) should be allowed to decide on war or peace, was settled long ago by the Poles in the affirmative sense".

"The principle according to which a people should have the right to order its own destiny was applied in Poland during a long period, even at the time when the absolute European monarchies were organizing armies that were forced to go to war by a single sign from their sovereign."

In 1496 the "general call to arms", that had up to that time depended on the King became an attribute of the Diet. After 1573— the time of the elaboraton of the first articles and pacts that were submitted to Henri de Valois—(before his election to the Polish throne) each monarch took oath not to declare war or order a general call without the authorization of the Diet. Thus it was the Diet alone that had the right to declare war, even though the war was to be fought by a mercenary army paid by the King. Such was the principle adopted by Polish law and that was maintained without fundamental change up to the very end of the existence of the Republic.

The peoples decision acted as a restraint and often prevented conflicts. This check was all the more powerful because of the people's repugnance for the slaughter of war. Poland guided by her strict moral principles held back, more than any other State, from useless bloodshed.

Before every declaration of war a commission was named in the Diet to examine into the more or less unavoidable character of the conflict, of the possibility of a peaceful settlement or the necessity to fight, and finally to decide on the legality of the Polish claims.

This idea of right and justice, that in international affairs seem like an anomaly, like a conception of another world, had a real value in the political life of the Polish State. Considering this as "one of the most important factors of life" the pedagogues instilled it into the minds of their scholars, with the first rudiments of the education that was to form their character. The Statute of the National Commission of Education, of 1773, charged the professors of history "never to call heroism or politics (the science of government) that which was only cunning, treason, baseness, violence, invasion and robbery"!

It is in vain that we look for another such official educational recommendation, not only in those times but even today. That declaration was the result of the very high level at which, for centuries, the notions of social life had been held in Poland.

Unfortunately in the presence of the general militarism of Europe and the rapacious instincts of other States, this high moral level of Poland brought about most deplorable consequences for her. That Poland was right—the Poland that had shrunk shuddering before the growing spectre of militarism,—that her principles responded to the needs of civilization and not to those that permitted the triumph of the enemies of the Republic, has been superabundantly proven by the fearful conflict of today into which "the wise and far-seeing Europe" allowed herself to be drawn.

———————o———————

X.

POLAND THE LIBERATOR.

THE SPREADING ABROAD OF LIBERTY.—THE LITHUANIAN NOBILITY BEFORE AND AFTER THE UNION WITH POLAND.—LADISLAS IV. AND THE CONSTITU- TION OF MOSCOVY.—EMIGRATION OF THE BOYARDS INTO POLAND.—THE ROLE OF THE POLES AFTER THE FALL OF STATE.—"FOR YOUR AND OUR LIBERTY."— ROLE OF POLAND IN THE WARS FOR FREEDOM.—THE UNIVERSALITY OF THE POLISH QUESTION.

Whenever Poland, during her long historic existence, entered into touch with other peoples, especially those that were weaker or little developed, she went not to shakle but to deliver them, not to subdue but to free them.

When, in 1611 after a long siege, the Polish armies entered Smolensk, a fortress that had been disputed by both Poles and Russians for a long time, a medal was struck at Warsaw having the following elequent inscription: "Dum vincor, libror". In truth, Smolensk retaken by the Poles was able to benefit once more by the great Polish liberties. Wherever Poland got a footing it was always the same, freedom was spread abroad and her liberties were felt by all. The justce of this affirmation is seen from the conditions under which all the unions between Poland and the neighboring coun- tries were carried through, from those made by the youthful State of the Piasts to those effected by the powerful monarchy of the Jagellons.

The "liberating" character of the Polish expansion was effec- tively shown when the nobility of the Prussian cities, oppressed by the Teutonic Order, placed themselves under the protection of Poland. Another proof is furnished by Livonia, which of her own free will joined the Polish Republic.

But by far the most remarkable testimony of the attraction of Polish freedom comes from Lithuania and Ruthenia. These two countries, at the moment of their union with Poland, were subject to the most cruel despotism under which all classes of the population

49

were weighed down. The Grand Duke, landowner of his State, had unlimited power. The Lithuanian and Ruthenian boyards ("bojary") could no more than a simple peasant dispose of their property or their family, nor could they even marry without the consent of their Prince.

The act of Union signed at Horodlo, in 1413, sets forth in a very clear and concise manner that: "the bonds of slavery that bind you shall be broken and the fetters shall be taken from you". From the first connections liberty was extended by Poland. Under the influences of the first unions absolute power was greatly restricted; the boyards were elevated to the rank of the Polish knights, individual rights were acquired, the right also to dispose of property, the land—whose use had depended on the good or ill-will of the Prince—became their own property. Marriage could take place without the authorization of the Prince and, finally, the boyard had the guarantee that he would not be condemned without having been judged according to law. Even the Oriental slavery endured by the Lithuanian peasant was changed into the moderated Western subjection then recognized in Poland.

The infiltration of Polish freedom into Lithuania continued for two hundred years. It was paralleled by the development of intellectual culture of which the principle home was the University of Cracow. Before the connections of the two States had become firm enough to allow of the real union of 1569, a phenomenon of assimilation and political kindredship had taken place between the internal organizations of the two countries.

Much before the time of the memorable "Diet of Lublin", the Lithuanian nobility had expressed their desire for this definite union, so that they might be free from the oligarchy of the magnates and come into full possession of all the liberties enjoyed by the Polish nobility. And these liberties that flowed so abundantly into the country, formerly subjected to despotism, continued there up to the very end of the political independence of the Republic.

Poland, after having broken the bonds of absolutism in Lithuania, extended her liberating mission farther to the East—into Moscovy. The influence of Poland on Moscovy began toward the end of the XVI. century, at the time when the Poles, going more and more frequently into the empire of the Czars, took with them their notions of the rights of the citizens and of constitutional government. "This contact with the Poles," writes Prince Peter Dolgorouky, "showed the boyards of Moscow to what a humiliating degree of slavery they were lowered, and made them see that in allowing themselves to become the plaything of their monarchs, they not only had to submit to tyranny but to bodily punishment as well".*

The first result of these Polish-Moscovite relations was an effort, made in 1605 to introduce into Moscow the same institutions that existed in Poland and to limit the absolute power of the Czar, Vladimir Shuisky (1605-1610). This Czar was required to swear solemnly never to arbitrarily confiscate property or condemn anyone to death without judgment. The election of Ladislas, the son of Sigismund III., to the throne of Moscovy, after the extinction of the Rurik dynasty, shows tangibly the desire of the Russians to enjoy the same liberties as then existed in Poland.

But it was only after 1610 that the ascendancy of the Republic over Moscovy reached its culminating point. Under the influence of the Polish political ideas and systems, Moscovy formed a representative organization composed of two chambers (the Duma of the Boyards and the Duma of the Rurals) without the sanction of which their sovereigns, just as in Poland, could not make any laws, increase the taxes, sign treaties or alliances, nor declare war. Moreover the Czar lost the right of suppression by capital punishment, of confiscation of property without lawful judgment, and an elective legislative corps was organized. A convention like the "pacta conventa" was passed between the Czar and the boyards.

When the shortsighted and insincere policies of Sigismund III. kept his son from ascending the Moscovite throne the boyards put the sceptre into the hands of Michel I. Romanoff. Then profiting by his youth the boyards forced him to recognize the constitutional government. This regime, however, lasted only six years because, in 1618, the Metropolite Filaret, the father of the new sovereign, released from captivity in Poland, became regent, took the power from the hands of the young Michel and put himself at the head of a reactionary government. Thus the Constitution that had hardly seen the light of day came to an end. However, up to the reign of Peter the Great, the "ukases" still bore the heading: "By order of the Czar with the consent of the boyards". But finally when Peter the Great came to the throne the last vestige of Russian Constitutionalism imported from Poland was wiped out.

The attraction of the Polish liberties was such that at the end of the XVI. century, one year after the "Union of Lublin", the in-

---

* Prince Peter Dolgarouky: Truth about Russia. Paris, 1860.

habitants of Novgorod decided to separate from Moscovy and demanded of the Republc to be united to Lithuania. But this design was foiled by Ivan the Terrible and drowned in waves of blood. Ivan could not, however, stop the emigration of the boyards who, one after the other, crossed the frontier into Poland never to return. "Like birds in the autumn," says Professor Waclaw Sobieski, "the boyards fleeing from the cold north sought a refuge in the country of freedom".* Like that Prince Kurbski, who, upon his arrival in Cracow, wrote the famous letter to the Czar in which he cursed the tyrant and threatened him with the Divine Wrath. Fifty years later when the first Romanoffs ascended the throne and the reform party disappeared under the oppression of the reactionaries, many more boyards, even abandoning their fortunes, sought refuge in Poland. At that time one branch of the family of Prince Soltykow emigrated into Poland and later gave to the country eminent patriots.

Up to the XVIII. century, every attempt, no matter how modest, to check absolutism was inspired by Polish institutions alone. Later they were inspired by the great French revolution. The conception of liberty, principal factor of political evolution, continued to spread among foreign peoples even after the downfall of the Republic. During the whole of the XIX century the Poles struggled on, at one time stirring up revolutionary currents and at another time offering their services to those who rose up against absolutism. But it was chiefly at home, among themselves, that they rose up against the detested despotism, at home that they incited a series of bloody insurrections to overthrow the tyrants who were oppressing them.

Notwithstanding their profound scorn for their persecutors they still felt some pity for them as well, because they considered them slaves blindly obedient to the conquering folly of their governments. In 1831 the Polish soldiers inscribed on their standards the watchword "for your and our liberty", watchword that reflected all the greaness of soul of historic Poland—that saw before all else, in each enemy, a miserable and degraded brother, and had only one desire: to lift him again to human dignity.

The Poles always joined the problem of their liberty with the liberty of the world; struggling against the oppression in their own country they felt themselves to be struggling at the same time for the happiness of other peoples and in fighting against despotism in any

---

* Waclaw Sobieski: The King and the Czar.

part of the world they felt they were struggling indirectly for the freeing of their own beloved Poland.

Every generation, since the partition of Poland, held to this tradition that started at the end of the XVIII. cenury. This inspired the two national heroes, Kosciuszko and Pulaski, when they offered their services to the starred flag of America. Pulaski fell on the battle field in America, Kosciuszko, after having rendered great services to the young American Republic, openly espoused, with Jefferson and Franklin the cause of the freedom of the slaves, to which Washington was opposed. Many Poles enrolled under the standards of Napoleon, proudly choosing the motto: "Gli Uomini Liberi son Fratelli" (all free men are brothers).

The Polish political emigrants of 1831 stimulated in their turn the activity of "young Europe". The years 1831 and 1848 saw Polish emigrants at every barricade and on every battle-field where independence was being fought for. These "Condottieri" of liberty, as the reactionaries disdainfully called them, went—soldiers, officers or generals—to fight in Italy, Hungary, in Germany and in Austria. It was the Polish General Miroslawski who put himself at the head of the insurrection in Baden and in Sicily; it was the Polish General Chrzanowski who commanded the army of Sardinia in Italy; it was the great poet, Adam Mickiewicz, who went to Milan with the Legion that he himself had formed to keep up the struggle to free all peoples. His watchword was only the extension of Christian principles from individual life to the life of nations. Among the Garibaldians there were also many Poles. At the head of the Vienna revolution was the Polish General Bem. Polish statesmen, Smolka and Goluchowski, soon opened the Constitutional Era. There were thousands of Poles enlisted in the revolutionary army of Hungary; General Dembinski was twice named "General-in-Chief" of these armies; another General, Wysocki, commanded a Polish legion and both he and General Bem covered themselves with glory in Transylvania. The Poles continued to fight although the Hungarians had lost all hope of victory.

In Ukraina the Polish insurrectionists, in 1863—noblemen mostly—proclaimed the "golden act" by freeing the Ruthenian peasants, although it was against the interests of the Polish agriculturists of the country. The same thing took place in Lithuania. Thus it was that the defenders of Europe against Eastern barbarism became after the downfall of their State, the champions of World-liberty. It was often at the price of Polish blood that the rights enjoyed today by free people, endowed with constitutional governments, were bought.

The political ideal, that emanated from subjected Poland and from her sons dispersed in foreign lands, explains why the Polish question, toward the middle of the XIX. century, took on its "character of universality". At that time young Europe began to see in the solution of this question the conditions of a general victory for liberty. The genius of the French people vividly felt the importance of this question and, after, 1831, for thirty years never left off by writings, by parliamentary discussions and by public manifestations, to push the war for Poland's freedom.

This popular, universal, political current in favor of the "Polish Cause", identified at the same time with all peoples, led the population of Berlin, in 1848, amid the greatest enthusiasm to carry the Polish patriots in triumph to the Royal Palace. The people of Europe, at that moment when their moral level was exalted to unknown heights, bowed before the spiritual force of this disowned and persecuted Poland.

Under the Empire the indescribable sufferings inflicted on Poland, and on the Polish soul, found a new force of resistance: it was the "ideal-force of the mystic conception that made of Poland the Christ of peoples, suffering as He suffered, for the salvation of humanity". This state of mind marked all the work of Poland's greatest romantic poets, Mickiewicz, Slowacki and Krasinski, magnificent work, with an extraordinary power of inspiration, born from the sufferings of their native country during the epoch of emigration.

This mission of liberators, that the Poles espoused, had its roots far back in the past. It was the logical consequence of the spiritual evolution of the old Republic, the result of the same spirit that in the olden time united "equals with equals and free with free". Guided by this motto, until then unknown, the Poles went into Lithuania and Ruthenia and thus realized in Eastern Europe, with extraordinary ease, their national ideal of social organization.

———————o———————

XI

POLAND IN ADVANCE OF CONTINENTAL EUROPE.

THE TREND OF POLITICAL DEVELOPMENT IN POLAND.—ABSOLUTISM IN EU-
ROPE AND CIVIL RIGHTS IN POLAND.—"REGNA SED NON IMPERA".—RESTRIC-
TION OF THE PRIVILEGES OF THE NOBILITY, ACCOMPLISHED BY THE NOBLES
THEMSELVES.—REVISION OF THE CONSTITUTION,—THE FEDERAL STATE.—
ACCOMPLISHMENT OF REFORMS WITHOUT REVOLUTION.—MORAL MATURITY.

In its development Poland was in advance of continental Europe
in many ways and by many years—centuries even. That which
other peoples did not demand of their governments until the XIX.
century, the Republic had centuries before instituted and guaranteed
by laws.

It was especially in the development of political rights that Poland was in advance of the other continental European States. Between the State as it was constituted in the middle ages and the
modern constitutional State, the annals of Poland did not have to
record the existence of that somber link called "enlightened
absolutism".

The transition from the medieval organization into the modern
parliamentary State was brought about with astonishing rapidity in
Poland. A few decades sufficed, while the rest of Europe took several centuries to attain the same end. Professor Stanislas Kutrzeba
states that, in this respect, the progress of Polish development was
far more logical than that of the West. The evolution of the
Polish Republic was in fact always characterized by a preponderance
—that became more and more marked—of popular elements, which
from the middle ages on sought power, and not without success;
while, in the meantime, in Western Europe these popular elements
were crushed by their respective monarchistic powers. As a result,
there is a deviation in the curve of the political development in
a contrary direction to that which it seemed to have taken at the
beginning; while in Poland, on the contrary, evolution continued to
follow the straight line—the line first laid down. Thus, Poland was
able to keep ahead of all the contemporary European States by her
organic structure—based on the union of monarchistic power and
the Diet—union that remains today one of the most essential and
valuable traits of the modern State.

When Europe had definitely entered into the period of absolutism, when the people had become the humble slaves of one master,

Poland was creating for herself institutions that guaranteed civic liberty, was developing a parliamentary system and improving her Diet that would soon be able to take over the greatest part of the power.

Toward the XVIII. century, when a serious need of reforms began to be felt, a Polish citizen, Wielhorski, applied to J. J. Rousseau asking his advice on reforms for the Republic. Rousseau answered the question by a long treatise * in which he demonstrated that the Polish organization was, on principle, excellent, and "worth more than that of Great Britain".

This is what von Rotteck, a German historian of Freiburg, says in his "General History" about "enlightened absolutism": "At that epoch science was the servant of despotism. With the exception of a few Republics, the pople were everywhere treated like flocks of sheep, and, in fact, it amounted to that in those countries where the will of the monarch was supreme and the sole aim was to satisfy the unlimited cupidity of princely families. At that time the greatest virtue was obedience". How much more advanced was the situation of Poland in the same epoch!

The security of individual liberty was protected by law. In this respect Poland was even ahead of the country classic for its individual freedom—England; for the Polish law "Neminem captivabimus" prescribing that no arrest could be made without proof of the guilt of the accused was enacted in 1430, that is to say, two and a half centuries before the famous "Habeas Corpus Act of 1679. As has been stated before, the principle of the publicity of debates—for the accusation as well as for the defense—was also known in Polish jurisdiction, a principle that existed nowhere else, except in England at that period. The people, through their representatives, decided the most important affairs of State, not excepting those relative to peace and war. The essentially republican form of government even placed the people in a position to elect the head of the State and gave to each citizen the possibility of one day becoming himself the King-President of the Republic.

The fundamental constitutional principles of the Republic, such as the law "nihil novi", the "pacta conventa" and the articles "non præstanda obœdientia", were inspired by the really modern conception that the King lived for the nation and not the nation for the King. The famous principle expressed by Thiers in 1831: "the King reigns but does not govern", for which the political science of

---

* J. J. Rousseau: Considerations on the Polish Government.

56

today prides itself, had already been laid down by the Polish politicians in 1607, two centuries before Thiers, in the same identical terms: "regna sed non impera".

With such institutions and such ideas there is nothing astonishing in the fact that Poland was able to leave the European States of her time far behind her, the epoch of which Rotteck says: "the people were considered as herds of cattle, and the King's word was all. It is true that by these liberties, created in the XVI. century and continued through the XVII. and XVIII. centuries, only one class benefited, but that class numbered a million souls. On the other hand, toward the end of the XVIII. century, Poland, again in advance of the greater part of Europe, undertook and brought to a successful end a great political reform and, although based on the already existing State organization, it ended the exclusive privileges of the nobility by extending the civic rights to other classes of the population, and adopted, at the same time, liberal institutions, fulfilling the ideas and requirements of the time.

This reform was the memorable Constitution of the 3rd of May, 1791.

Adhering to the spirit of Polish traditions, the law of May 3rd was based on the principle that "in human society all power springs from the will of the people". The application of this political conception resulted in the creation of a Ministry responsible to the Diet. From then on, when laws were broken, the Diet could accuse the Ministry and when the representatives and the government disagreed, the Diet could demand the dismission of the Ministry providing that the majority of the opposition amounted to two-thirds of the representative body. Thus Poland, at that time, applied the principle that is still today unrecognized in some constitutional States: that the government cannot exercise its power unless it is upheld by the parliamentary majority of the representative body.

From the social and political point of view, the Polish constitution of 1791 took from the nobility the greater part of their privileges; at the same time it enlarged this class by admitting into it new elements of society. The right of ennoblement was, one may say, automatically acquired by all those who paid a certain minimum of land tax, and to officers and certain categories of officials. Besides, each Diet was obliged to ennoble a certain number of the middle class who had distinguished themselves in different domains, especially commerce and industry. The old conception of nobility was quite abolished and every citizen having a certain social standing was eligible to nobility.

The nobility was thus transformed into a republican middle class in the largest sense of the word, and the remarkable perspective opened of the gradual ennoblement of all the people.

The middle classes of the cities, as a whole, were what might be called half ennobled: they were given the right of "neminem captivabimus", access to all civil and military honors, a large autonomy, the right to become landowners—a concession made only in 1807, or sixteen years later in Prussia—and lastly, greater access to the Diet. From then on all work, no matter whether carried on in the cities or in the fields, had the right to the same respect. In sign of fraternity the greatest dignitaries allowed their names to be inscribed in the municipal registers.

Lastly, the peasant class, named in one of the articles of the new code as "the most valiant force of the country" were taken under the protection of the law. Although the situation of the middle classes and the peasants was far from perfect, the reformers did not go farther, convinced with reason that to become lasting, reforms should progress slowly. It should be noted that this constitution, all to the disadvantage of the nobles, was framed by a Diet made up exclusively of the nobility and without any compulsion from the other less favored classes.

The remarkable characteristic of this Constitution was that the new reforms were intended for the present generation only. Although they were greatly in advance of their times, these laws had not been elaborated to become enduring but were only to serve as steps to the future development of the country. Recognizing the necessity to revise this Constitution, "after having judged its effects upon public prosperity", it was decided that a special Diet should meet every twenty-five years and proceed with the revision of the laws. The deep wisdom of the authors of those reforms of May 3rd was manifested in a striking manner by the additional law that ordered the following generation to adapt the organization of the State to the new ideas and new exigencies. The application of this law would have been a powerful help to the Polish people toward reaching their ideal of liberty. And that liberty would eventually have been extended to all classes, if the partitions had not put a brutal end of this evolution.

By this Constitution of May 3rd, 1791, as by all her previous evolution, Poland, as we have seen, was in advance of a number of the great European peoples that were subject to autocratic governments. Even more, because of this wise legislation that prescribed periodic revisions of the Constitution, the Polish Republic was in advance of many States of even the present day.

In a second domain, we see yet again the superiority of the Polish political genius in comparison to that of other continental European States. It was their skill in organizing the life of the different peoples making up the Republic. Several centuries before the creation of the American union—a model of political organization uniting, for the common good, elements of different origin and culture—Poland created a great Federation of peoples in Europe.

The unions with Lithuania, Ruthenia, the Prussia of Dantzig and Livonia transformed the small State of the Piasts into a great Federal Power. Although each of these peoples were possessed of the strictest autonomy, although they were united only by the two central organs—the Diet and the King—their cohesion was such that even the downfall of the Republic did not destroy it. And the political work accomplished by Poland remains unequaled, even up to the present time.

Quite incomparable also were the means used by the State to reach the goal she had in view. The two fundamental reforms—the law of 1515 "nihil novi", that was the starting point of the parliamentary and political liberties and the Constitution of May 3rd, 1791, that adapted these liberties to the needs of the time—were realized without any revolutionary disturbance and without the shedding of one drop of blood. "That which other people," said Stephen Buszczynski, "had aspired after through long centuries, and had only reached through blood and massacres, regicides and scaffolds, the Polish people had won and held by legal means and in all tranquility". And even thus, by way of peaceful evolution and through the wisdom of her statesmen and the attraction of her political freedom, these different *unions were accomplished*: the federation of several peoples *without the help of sword* or diplomatic cunning. The superiority of this method of political construction was on a par with the moral superiority of the Poles over their neighbors near and far.

The State that instructed its youth that politics was not synonomous with cunning, treachery or violence, that, notwithstanding the prevailing preponderance of rapacious instincts, avoided wars of conquest on principle, that examined into the justice of each war, that in the midst of general fanaticism was the only example of religious toleration in Europe, that could not persecute people for their faith or their origin, that had never assassinated their Kings but who did not allow their Kings to murder their subjects, that attached more importance to the renown of their laws than to the Crown, that loathed all extortion, and that gave freedom to the neighboring peoples—such a State was morally, incontestably, in advance of the Europe of yesterday, and of the Europe of today, by the whole length of her historic existence.

———————o———————

XII.

THE DOWNFALL OF THE POLISH STATE.

INQUIRIES INTO THE CAUSE OF THE DOWNFALL.—ANARCHY AND ABSENCE OF JUSTICE. "VITAL INCAPACITY" CREATING A MODEL CONSTITUTIONAL STATE.—FOR WHOM DID POLISH ANARCHY CONSTITUTE A DANGER?— POLAND VICTIM OF PHYSICAL VIOLENCE.

The Polish State had come to an end. For people who judge principles and acts by their immediate success, this fact was sufficient to disprove the course by which the development of Poland had been accomplished.

"But it is not the hand of man that regulates the clock of history"....The political organization that during long centuries was a source of prosperity and high culture to a great people; the genius of Polish history, that inspired entire generations with ardent patriotism, by inciting them to resist heroically every persecution and all suffering, the ideal, so profoundly human, of freedom and of dignity toward which the efforts of all nations tend, no! that could not have been the cause of all the suffering and misfortune that fell on Poland.

Today the Polish people believe, as Buszczynski said, "that their role among nations is only interrupted—not ended".

The events that brought about the downfall of the Polish State have been the subject of a great many learned discussions. The authors of the partitions were the first to feverishly seek after these causes. The greatest faith was put in a thesis that was zealously pushed forward for a long time and that even at the present day is still in circulation, like the proverbial "bad coin", in the mist of opinions. This is the thesis of the official Russian historiographers who pretended that Poland fell because of anarchy and of "internal incapacity" to live as a State. This story forged by perfidy and carried on by stupidity has, in the course of time, taken on the character of an accusation pronounced from the height of a would-be historical tribunal.

But who are they, that feel thus warranted to accuse the past of Poland of anarchy? Even those in whose countries for centuries no laws existed and who a hundred-fold more than "the Polish anarchy", should be subject to the severe judgment of history.

At the most unfortunate period of Polish evoluion—during the reign of the Wettin dynasty of Saxony—the existence of an executive power, strong enough to enforce the strict application of the laws was lacking, but the laws themselves never fell into disuse and never lost their force. At the same period Russia had no notion of law. The least sign or desire of their sovereigns became law even when these signs came from a bloody maniac like Ivan the Terrible, or strumpets like Catherine II. of Anhalt-Zerbst.

And who is it that speaks thus of our "incapacity to live?" Even those whose vitality was manifested by spoilation and rapine and the humility of dogs under the lash. It is a shameless lie to assert that vitality is synonymous with slave-servility and rapacious instincts. It will be enough to cite two facts to invalidate such accusations.

The final organization of the Republic was maintained through three centuries; in consequence, it must have possessed a certain vitality, especially since it was supported in a very slight degree only, by the restraint exercised by the State. The second and third partitions of Poland went into effect at a time when Poland adapting herself to the new ideas and needs of the time had instituted the reforms of May 3rd, 1791—at a time when by its organization and laws it could be called a model State. This testifies in a striking manner that Poland was capable of development.

Anarchy was one of the causes of our downfall but not the anarchy generally understood as such. The nature of the Polish Constitution that had become changed and degenerated through the course of time still, however, had a foundation of sound and fertile ideas even at the time of the worst disorders (for example, the exaggerated conception of individual rights carried to the extreme in the "liberum veto"). Now, these ideas of freedom carried over the frontiers might have become dangerous to the absolutism that reigned abroad.

"Is it necessary to search farther for the cause of the partitions of Poland?" asks, with reason, Buszczynski, "this great country, truly democratic was an anomaly among neighboring dynastic states.

61

Poland, notwithstanding her decline and although apparently in her death struggle, showed at least as strong a vitality as the European monarchies, with all their martial uproar and the magnificence of their courts. Everywhere in Europe the people were only things—the blind instruments of him who was strongest and the most clever. While in Poland the people had never been slaves to their Kings."

The neighboring powers saw in the Constitution of the Republic (especially in the reforms of May, 1791) a dangerous example for their "subjects" forced to blind obedience. And the more it was feared, Polish Jacobism was all the more open to criticism. Autocracy, that had already been sapped by France, would continue to run the risk of being threatened by Poland, if her re-establishment was not opposed. This danger had to be eliminated at all costs. Hence the partitions.

Poland fell because she was not in unison with her neighbors, and *because,* instead of restraining her citizens, *she enlarged their rights.* Poland fell guilty of having a political organization more liberal, more developed, more perfect, than the neighboring powers. This was the "primary cause" of her disappearance from the map of Europe. But on the other hand, her downfall was brought about by the terrible ring encircling her, that hemmed her in and against which she was powerless to struggle.

A great people—a people who had rendered immense service to civilization—that had never cherished hostile sentiments against anyone was surrounded in the very center of Europe, and hunted like a beast. A thing without precedent in the history of peoples.

An examination of this unheard of situation leaves room, doubtless, for the critic to blame Polish politicians who were unable to draw the country from this trap by improving the diplomatic situation of the country. But to the critic one may reply by bringing to mind the existence of the alliance made in 1791 by Poland with the Western Powers and which was *cynically and ruthlessly broken* and trampled upon by them. Poland was confronted by a formidable plot and succumbed to the preponderant force of the three neighboring powers—victim of physical violence she fell as Prussia fell, under exactly the same circumstances, after the battle of Jena. Prussia, however, was a completely " militarized" State.

———————o———————

XIII.

THE SIGNIFICANCE OF POLISH HISTORY AT THE PRESENT TIME.

THE RESULTS OF THE PARTITION OF POLAND.—DESTRUCTION OF EQUILIB-
RUM.—THE DOWNFALL OF POLAND AND ITS RELATION TO THE PRESENT
DAY.—POPULARIZATION OF THE IDEA OF VIOLENCE.—DEVELOPMENT OF MIL-
ITARISM.—THE WORLD WAR.—THE REPRESSION OF THE INDIVIDUAL.—
HISTORICAL POLAND AND CONTEMPORARY EUROPE.

Poland was struck from the map of Europe. This violent suppression of a great State, full of vitality, whose only aspiration was toward development, had ill-fated consequences for the whole system of European connections.

In a note to Metternich, in 1814, Talleyrand expressed the opinion that the dismemberment of Poland was the cause of all the commotion that followed in Europe. Von Rotteck, that remarkable German historian already quoted, wrote ninety years ago:

"The downfall of Poland proclaimed in a voice of thunder the total overthrow of European equilibrum, the victorious reign of violence and the utter destruction of international rights." According to the profound words of Johann von Muller: "God would reveal the moral value of the powers of the world; a somber future appeared to thinkers, showing them the advent of infinite distress and the prospect of appalling consternation, needful for the reestablishment of right and justice." Today, these prophetic words have found their terrible confirmation.

For minds that see into the heart of things it is evident that between the great international crime of the partitions of Poland and the monstrous conflict of today, there is the undeniable relation of cause and effect. Lord Eversley states in his recently published book * that *the partitions of Poland*, although remote and indirect, *are the essential cause of the great World War*. The crimes committed against Poland, the tortures that were systematically inflicted upon her, have had disastrous consequences on the Europe of the XIX. and XX. centuries.

When the autocratic powers combined against the French Revolution, Poland was no longer able to go to the aid of the French, although her traditional love of liberty, her republican and democratic organization, her cult for the rights of the individual and the

---

* The Partition of Poland.

sovereignty of the people responded to the ideas proclaimed by
Revolutionary France.

Napoleon, who changed the nature of the ideals of the Revolution but adopted their principles and spread them broadcast over
Europe, *admitted* in his "memoires" that *his greatest error was in
not having revived Poland.* After the fall of Napoleon the authors
of the partitions laid at the Congress of Vienna the base of the
"Holy Alliance", that was for thirty years to smother every liberal
idea, hinder the development of peoples and thus leave such a deplorable impression on the whole of the XIX. century.

The attempts to justify the crime of which Poland was the
victim, corrupted the minds and moral sense of the peoples, slavery
and tyranny imposed on a nation made the idea of violence common-
place and the realization of the desires of despotic governments, who
were using this vigorous method with their own "subjects", was
made easier. Then, the States hastened to enlarge their military
forces, some because they feared the fate of Poland, and others because they were tempted by aggressive policies, to satisfy their ap-
petites whetted by the acquisition of Poldand....All this: antago-
nisms awakened by the division of the spoils, the immoderate increase of one on the ruins of others, the building up of the gigantic
Russia on the ashes of Poland; all this was the supreme reason for
the universal armament, so characteristic of the XIX. century.

"Russia with millions of servile people at her disposition,"
writes Professor Waclaw Sobieski, "could, because of the partitions
of Poland, advance far into Europe; she advanced yet farther in
1815, and reached its very heart, in 1831, after having crushed the
Polish army. In place of the old Republic, that had no wish to keep
up a standing army, it was Russia that entered the lists and spread
terror by the continual onward movement of her troops and forced
the neighboring States to put themselves on guard and keep up their
standing armies.

The partitions of Poland hastened in yet another way the armaments. Every violent conquest necessitates watchfulness over the
occupied territories and the subjection of the vanquished population
—especially of a population so imbued with freedom as the Poles
were. The German military writer, Max Jahns,* expressly declares
that "Prussia was forced to enlarge its armies because of the occupation of the Polish Republic". Frederic William II., in 1795, insti-

---

* Max Jahns—Heeresverfassungen und Völkerleben.

tuted a "Commission of Military Organization"* that not only felt the need of enlarging the army but also of instituting a general recruitment.

The exhaustion caused by the Napoleonic wars was not yet over when it became necessary to apply themselves to watching the Poles who waited only a favorable moment to regain their freedom.

Nicholas I. could not master his impatience or his anger when he exclaimed: (1831) "only to keep the Poles in hand I am obliged, at great expense, to maintain a whole army".

The advance made by the Russians west of the Vistula, after 1831, filled the Prussians with such concern that, contrary to their custom, instead of disbanding the conscripts after their term of service, they kept them under the colors two years longer.

When the principle of nationalities and of national unions appeared in Europe, electrifying once again the Poles, Alexander II. put four army corps on a war-footing and re-enforced all the garrisons in Poland. These measures did not fail to awaken the distrust of Prussia. The Prussian Regent, William, mobilized troops at random (1859), doubled his permanent army, lengthened the duration of military service and made it obligatory.

These are facts that prove in an obvious manner the recoil of the dismemberment of Poland on the development of contemporary militarism. As Lord Eversley says, "the armed peace—an indirect but essential consequence of the subjection of a great people—becoming amplified by other factors, has in the course of time taken on huge dimensions and hindered the progress of civilization of all the peoples of Europe".

The States, each and all, armed themselves and the world in truth, became a stage for "a competition of armaments".

The greater part of the population, from the social point of view, was turned from productive work. The budgets destined for the development of industry, of public instruction and hygiene were notably reduced in favor of military budgets; that more and more consumed. the State revenues.

The course followed by the European States, after the downfall of Poland, so authoritatively described by von Rotteck, "led the powers to keep six million men under arms, condemning them to inactivity during the strength of their manhood". It is the people who have been obliged to furnish these six million men and it has been the people who have been charged with the up keep of these armies,

---

* Immediat-Militär Organisations-Kommission.

costing billions. And finally, this State militarism has ended in the monstrous massacre that has covered the whole of Europe with blood and destroyed so much of what had been created by human activity during generations.

This cataclysm has surpassed all preconceptions: at the end of the third year forty million men have been called to arms, at an expense of three hundred billion francs; there have been five million men killed, twelve million more wounded and three and a half million invalided....The civilian mortality behind the lines increases in a terrifying manner. "The infinite distress" that Charles von Rotteck foresaw is an accomplished fact.

Sobs are choking millions of breasts; millions of families have lost their support, the spectre of death advances over the ruined cities and villages. The spectre of famine rises up threatening the Europe that yesterday was so proud of her wealth. The sacrifices that war imposes on all peoples surpass imagination.

The obligation to make everything subordinate to the aims of war extends to all domains of life. The individual has been repressed to an inconceivable degree, until he has become nothing but the wheel of a monstrous engine.

Under the empire of the instinct of self-preservation, humanity can only face with horror the possibility of a renewal of such a catastrophe. She demands the revision of the system that has caused such disaster, the institutions of tribunals of arbitration, that being subject to international control will decide disputes, and lastly the elaboration of an international penal code, according to which every attempt to disturb the peace will be considered as the greatest crime.

And now, just one more glance backward.

In the perspective of time we see the resplendent Polish Republic; in the olden time so full of vitality and later so brutally destroyed. But in the Polish heart this Republic has never ceased to live—this Republic that two centuries ago had already realized many dreams of modern humanity, that never manifested rapacious instincts, that detested all shedding of blood, that instructed her parliament to decide on war and peace, that put real value on the conception of equity in the rules of international relationships, that gave the name of "Great" to Kings who were "constructors" and not to Kings who were "plunderers", that taught the young not to confound treachery with politics or heroism with violence, that never persecuted people for their origin or their faith,

66

that freed people and confederated them maintaining the equality of rights, that was an island of freedom in the midst of a sea of absolutism, that respected the rights of the individual; that placed Law above the Crown, that was centuries in advance of other States, not only in realizing the different principles for which they struggled later on, but also, in realizing a number of those that other peoples are only just now beginning to foresee.

Considering all these original creations emanating from the political genius of the Polish people, we can now understand, face to face with the appalling reality, what humanity has lost by the disappearance of the Polish State and how greatly the absence of Poland's help has been felt in the realization of the common aims toward which civilization tends.

Lightning Source UK Ltd.
Milton Keynes UK
10 June 2010

155380UK00001B/11/P